MOISTURE DAMAGE 12/02

P9-DFP-311

REDNECK NATION

REDNECK NATION

How the South Really Won the War

MICHAEL GRAHAM

WARNER BOOKS

An AOL Time Warner Company

Warner Books, Inc., 1271 Avenue of the Americas, New York, NY 10020

Visit our Web site at www.twbookmark.com.

 An AOL Time Warner Company

Printed in the United States of America

First Printing: October 2002
10 9 8 7 6 5 4 3 2 1

Library of Congress Cataloging-in-Publication Data

Graham, Michael
     Redneck nation : how the South really won the war / Michael Graham.
        p. cm.
     ISBN 0-446-52884-6
     1. United States—Politics and government—2001—Humor. 2. United States—
Politics and government—1993-2001—Humor. 3. United States—Social life and
customs—1971—Humor. 4. Southern States—Politics and government—1951—
Humor. 5. Southern States—Social life and customs—1865—Humor. 6. Graham,
Michael, 1963—Anecdotes. I. Title.

E902.G73 2002
973'.02'07—dc21   2002071339

To my father, Simon Graham of Horry County, SC, who taught me never to trust a Yankee; and to my mother, Patricia Futrell Graham of Los Angeles, CA, who told me that nothing good ever came out of the South.

You were both right.

Contents

Introduction

My first college roommate at Oral Roberts University was John, a thirty-seven-year-old captain in the Nigerian Army. We were thrown together in one of those inexplicable twists of fate that are, for me, indisputable truth that there is a God and He writes for Monty Python.

I was an eighteen-year-old white kid straight from the rural South. A graduate of the South Carolina public school system, I came to Oral Roberts because of a deep, spiritual calling to attend whatever university was farthest from South Carolina and offered me a full scholarship. That's how I ended up in the shadow of the Prayer Tower in Tulsa, Oklahoma.

John spoke seven languages, none of them English. At least, not that I could tell. And though he was an officer in a national army that regularly fired on its own citizens without apology, John himself was a gentle, almost gregarious man. That fact did not lessen the shock a southern white boy feels on his first morning away from home when he is awakened at dawn by a large black man in Nigerian cammies doing anticommunist calisthenics at the foot of his bed.

John had never been to America before. His knowledge of our country came almost entirely from his exposure to commercial television back in Africa. And so our first conversation went something like this:

JOHN: Where were you born, Michael?
ME: Los Angeles, California.
JOHN: California! Hollywood, movie stars!
ME: How do you like it here in Oklahoma?
JOHN: Oklahoma! Cowboys, Indians, Wild West! So where do you live now?
ME: Actually, I grew up down in South Carolina . . .
JOHN: South Carolina! The American South! Dixie! Ah, the South, ahem . . . Oh. I see.

Later that night, I found him checking my pillowcases for eyeholes.

Here's a guy from Africa who doesn't know Montana from Maryland and thinks Walt Disney was one of our greatest presidents, but he knows enough about the South to assume that every white guy from South Carolina is in the KKK.

I didn't think much of this southern stereotyping at the time because I was used to it. In fact, not only was I unfazed by charges that white southerners were racist, redneck hicks, I was an enthusiastic witness for the prosecution.

There is no other way to put it: I hated growing up in the South. From the age of six, I lived in the rural town of Pelion, South Carolina, a picturesque community of 211 hearty southern folk, where I spent my formative years running from large, hairy people named "Bubba," many of them women.

The public school was a single campus that accommodated all twelve grades, so I spent my entire educational career with the same group of drawling, intellectually uninspired mouth-breathers, most of whom thought I was a pinhead who read too many books.

The students didn't like me, either.

I spent my summers cropping tobacco in the Pee Dee region of South Carolina, home of NASCAR's Darlington International Speedway and one of America's highest rates of sexually transmitted diseases, which, due to local cultural traditions, would often spike immediately after large family reunions.

It was during one of these summers working tobacco that I learned how powerful racism was as a social force in the South: A black coworker pulled a knife on me late one afternoon in one of the sweltering tobacco barns. Back then the barns were tall, narrow, heat-holding structures with huge rails—skinned tree trucks, actually—used for hanging sticks of green tobacco while they cured. My black assailant was only half serious and we were both very young and who knows if we were on the verge of a fight or a tutorial on fingernail cleaning, but when the knife appeared, the same redneck barn workers who had tortured me throughout the summer began dropping from the railings above to rescue me. They seemed to appear out of thin air, like Army Rangers dropping from Black Hawks in a firefight.

After beating the crap out of the black field worker and his friends, one of the older boys in the group looked at me and, seeing the wonder across my face, said, "Don't worry—we still hate you, too."

To this day, I think he meant it in a nice way.

Back home, my family and I attended a series of small

evangelical churches, the kind where the casting-out of demons was a regularly scheduled part of services. These were old-time, red-meat "Thank you, Jesus!" southern churches with a Pentecostal flair. I never attended a church with a mainstream name: no First Baptist or Elm Street Methodist. No, we always seemed to be the newest members of places called Springdale Revival Center or Shekinah Temple or God's Gonna Smite Yo' Ass-embly of God.

And so I grew up going to church four or five times a week and playing "fuhtbawl" and hunting squirrels and getting called "nigger lover" and having the Great American Southern White Boy Experience. All that was missing was a banjo and severe dental problems.

Which is why I never complained when Northerners (or Nigerians) cracked wise about me or my homeland. When I saw movies or TV shows mocking the South as an inbred backwater of racial obsession, good-ol'-boy politics, and *Hee Haw* culture, I didn't grouse because I knew they were right. All I had to do was look around my living room.

But I also inferred that these Northerners who were looking down on us were doing so because they were different. I just assumed they mocked southern ideas and attitudes because they, as Northerners, found them at the least strange, at the most repulsive, and, under any circumstances, unacceptable.

So it threw me off my stride when, less than fifteen minutes after arriving in Boston, Massachusetts, for the first time, the very first white person I spoke to used the word "nigger."

I had just pulled into town and needed directions. I

stopped at a gas station where a burly, blue-shirted white guy with his name over the pocket barked at me (or is that "baaked" at me), "You're all turned around, buddy. This is Nigger Town."

My head almost snapped back. Here I was, eight hundred miles north of the redneck wonderland I had fled in rural South Carolina, and the first Yankee I talk to is a racist idiot. I couldn't believe it. Then I saw him glance at my out-of-state license plate. "Aha," I thought to myself, "he's just going native on me as a southerner. It's really my fault," I told myself in a pathetically codependent way.

And in a way, it *was* my fault. I spent six years doing stand up comedy, traveling to forty-one states and performing for thousands of people; I spent six more years working as a GOP political consultant in places like Chicago and Westchester County, New York, talking to volunteers and voters from both sides of the political aisle. And inevitably I found that not only did northerners assume I was a closet Klan member but they had my tacit permission to slip on the intellectual white sheet as well.

In 1997, I was at a cocktail party in Westchester County, which is ground zero for limousine liberalism in America, the kind of place where Bill Clinton's annoying mix of self-absorption and self-righteousness would fit right in. Surrounded by Manhattan expatriates, SUV socialites, and liberals with causes, I happened to mention that I'm from South Carolina. It turns out one of the gathered had gone through army basic training at Fort Jackson in Columbia. Without so much as a sidelong glance, he tells me:

"I like you southerners. You sure know how to handle your niggers."

I have since discovered that incidents like these are

hardly the exception. Yes, I realize that anecdotes alone aren't sufficient for drawing grand conclusions about society north of the Mason-Dixon line. But after a lifetime fleeing my southern heritage and looking for that place in America that practices (for the lack of a better term) "Northernism," I am persuaded that no such place exists. As Gertrude Stein said of Oakland, there is no there there.

I've eaten Maxwell Street hot dogs near Chicago's Cabrini Green, Norwegian *lefse* in Minnesota, sturgeon from the Columbia River, lobster rolls in Massachusetts, ribs in Kansas City, homemade salsa in Los Angeles, and mounds of fries and gravy at the diner around the corner from the Improv in New York.

I've driven through the Rockies a half dozen times, gotten into arguments with snot-nosed college pukes on the steps of a Boston comedy club, suffered through a program of awful Italian folk songs sung in worse Italian by Sicilian wanna-bes in Yonkers, New York, and had a shotgun pulled on me at a gas station in Umatilla, Washington.

I've written two books, been on dozens of TV shows, and debated everyone from Alan Dershowitz to Pat Buchanan on my talk radio program. I've spent my entire adult life critiquing American politics, culture, society, and the arts from virtually every corner of this country. At every stop, I was looking for that place so far and so distinct from the Land of Cotton, that corner of America where the old times of the South would finally be forgotten. And guess where I am today, my northern American Yankee friend?

Right back where I started from, smack-dab in the heart of Dixie.

Twenty years of traveling, tracking, seeking, and soul-searching, and I have come to the horrifying conclusion that there is no escape. I'm Dustin Hoffman in *Papillon*. I'm never getting out because there is no out to get.

I live in a Redneck Nation.

From Bangor, Maine, to Baja, California; from Washington State to West Palm Beach; from the ever-burning lights of Manhattan, New York, to the never-ending boredom of Manhattan, Kansas; from the campuses of Hahvahd, Mass., to the cubicles of Chicago's high-rises: No matter where you go in this American nation, you will be surrounded, beset, and overwhelmed by redneckery.

Forget the calzone and cannoli; the only real difference between Brooklyn, New York, and Birmingham, Alabama, is that you can't get a gun rack into a Trans Am.

Every one of the fundamental southern ideas I spent my life opposing—racism, irrationalism, mysticism, professional wrestling—has been accepted and absorbed by our nation as a whole. It's as if Jefferson Davis came back to life to lead a black helicopter Confederate coup, seized control of the Union, and took command of the airwaves . . . but everyone was too dumb to notice.

Yes, Northerners and Southerners talk differently, and, yes, we eat differently and vote differently and express our arguments differently, but the same Old South principles are at work. Somehow—and I'll be damned if I can figure it out—the South lost the Civil War of 1860, lost the civil rights struggle of 1960, but has managed to win the battle of ideas.

This is not a good thing. The South is a land of few ideas, nearly all of them bad.

And if you're a typical modern northern American, they are probably yours.

1

Joe Lieberman, Redneck

When Al Gore announced his pick of Senator Joe Lieberman as his running mate for the 2000 election, we Southerners felt the cold, unfriendly glare of the northern media establishment on the back of our necks. The first Jewish candidate joins a major party's national ticket, and immediately the editorialists look southward over their reading glasses and demand, "Well?"

The Associated Press headlined a Karin Miller story "How Will Lieberman Play in the South?" Ron Brownstein of the *Los Angeles Times* wrote, without source or attribution, "If there is any backlash against Lieberman, it's most likely to come among Southern evangelical Protestants in states Gore will probably lose anyway."

Al Gore himself, praising his own courage and vision, insisted that by simply nominating Lieberman he would "tear down a mighty wall of division." The location of this mighty wall was undisclosed, but it's a safe bet he believed it to be somewhere south of Skokie, Illinois.

Joe Lieberman: welcomed candidate in the North, suspected Christ killer in the South. That was the story. But this time, the media right-thinkers were all wrong.

I say this as an avid practitioner of southern self-hatred who under normal circumstances is more than happy to give my homeland a swift kick in the crawdads. I know from firsthand experience that racism, ignorance, and idiocy down South aren't as bad as you think: They're worse.

In fact, I am so openly critical of my homeland that the natives have awarded me the premier appellation for disloyal Southerners: scalawag. (The South is the only region of America with a vocabulary dedicated solely to describing its infidels.) A scalawag is any white southern male (we would never use such a rude word for a lady) who opposes the official flying of the Confederate flag, supports the activities of the NAACP, or uses an excessive amount of noun-verb agreement.

I plead guilty. But on the issue of southern anti-Semitism, I must defer to the facts. For example:

Where is the oldest synagogue building in the United States in continuous use? What is the home of the fourth oldest Jewish congregation in America? Boston? Philadelphia? New York? No, Charleston. Charleston, South Carolina. (The third oldest congregation is in that northern enclave of Savannah, Georgia.)

Who was the first Jewish U.S. senator in America? Judah P. Benjamin of Louisiana. Yes, the home of Dixieland and David Duke: Louisiana. In 1852—when he would have been kicked out of every "decent" club in Connecticut or Massachusetts—Judah P. Benjamin was representing the very southern folks of Louisiana as a member of America's most exclusive debating society. After the secession, the reviled white Protestants of the Confederacy went kosher and chose Benjamin to serve in the national cabinet as secretary of war and later secretary of state.

In my home state of South Carolina, the building that houses the offices of our state representatives is the Solomon Blatt Building. Blatt, the son of poor Jewish immigrants, served in the House for fifty-four years—right through Jim Crow and the rise of the KKK. For thirty three of those years, which included the tumultuous era of the Civil Rights Movement, he served as Speaker. Indeed, when the Confederate battle flag was first raised over the statehouse, it was under the watchful eye of Speaker Sol Blatt.

According to southern scholar John Shelton Reed of the University of North Carolina, if the American South today were a nation, it would have the sixth largest Jewish population in the world. Include Jews from *outside* Palm Beach, Florida, and that ranking jumps even higher.

But the point is still made: Jews in America, both at the founding of Charleston's Beth Elohim temple in 1742 and in the Florida condominiums of today, have found the South at least as hospitable as the rest of the nation.

And yet northern newsrooms covering the 2000 election operated under the unexamined assumption that the closed-minded South is an enclave of Jew haters, while the open-minded North is a bastion of tolerance and acceptance. Are there anti-Semites down in Dixie? You might as well ask if there are anti-Semites in Brooklyn. Or Brookline. Or Chicago. (Just ask Congressman Rahm Emmanuel.)

My personal experience as a Southerner raised in a strongly evangelical home who attended Oral Roberts University is that I never encountered anti-Semitism—in word or deed—while growing up in the South. Yes, Al Gore and Joe Lieberman lost every southern state in 2000 (including Gore's humiliating loss in Tennessee), but they didn't lose a single one of these states because of the senator's faith in Jehovah.

As for Gore/Lieberman's faith in big-government liberalism . . . well, that's another matter.

With this clear, objective record, why is the South viewed in such a negative light, compared to the rest of America? To the typical nonSoutherner, we're still the twenty-first-century equivalent of the swimming club in Great Neck, New York, that refused to let Groucho Marx join because he was Jewish. ("Well, then, how about my son?" asked Groucho. "He's only *half* Jewish. Can he go in up to his waist?")

I stand today and accuse you, my northern friends, not of antisouthern prejudice, but of worse: snobbery. Snobbery and self-righteousness, both of which are unexamined and undeserved. The typical American Northerner, when considering his Southerner neighbors, suffers under what can best be described as "delusions of adequacy."

As a white Southerner who has spent much of his life traveling America, I have repeatedly experienced the immediate, visceral snobbery that northern Americans, particularly liberals from urban centers, emote when they meet Southerners. It's an unpleasant mix of suspicion and condescension. You shake our hands cautiously and, after a "Who bought you the shoes?" glance at our clothes, give a dubious smile as though you expect us to burst into an enthusiastic rendition of "Dixie" or start asking questions about how to work the indoor toilet.

It's not that there aren't plenty of real southern rednecks a videotape of my last family reunion could have been a *National Geographic* special titled "Swimming the Shallow End of the Gene Pool: Redneck Reproduction in the American Southeast." And I will never dispute the notion that the American South is dominated by irrational attitudes about race, religion, and culture. My challenge is: Tell me what part of America *isn't.*

This smugness, this condescension, this false sense of superiority that you Northerners feel toward me and my fellow Southerners, is the reason I wrote this book. Believe me, I grew up believing Northerners were the erudite, rational, antiracist advocates of achievement and culture you pretend to be. It took me twenty years to find out you were lying.

I know that many readers, Southerners in particular, will reject the idea that there is any significant demarcation of America, North and South. That the South is the stupidest place in America is obviously, palpably true, but when it comes to the truth, most Southerners are like the jury in the O. J. Simpson trial. We will not be influenced by mere facts.

But this isn't a regional conflict between bagels and biscuits. What I thought was happening in the 1960s during the civil rights struggle was a cultural battle between two worldviews, "Northernism" and "Southernism."

And there is a distinct southern culture. I lived the southern life, I was enveloped in the southern spirit, I drank from the deep springs of southern pride, and, at my first opportunity, I ran like a bat out of hell.

Let me be clear: I didn't just leave the South. I rejected it. As a teenager, whenever I met people for the first time, I would always try to work in the phrase "Well, I was *born* in Los Angeles . . ." The fact that I didn't know Compton from Santa Clarita was irrelevant. It gave me that one measure of distance from my southern identity.

When I was thirteen, my father played a cassette recording he had made of me speaking to the church. I think it was "Kids Who Found Christ Through Herbalife" Day or something like that, and I was working the crowd hard—but that *voice*. Ugh! I sounded like an adolescent Jethro Clampett addressing the annual belt buckle collectors' convention. Imagine a cross between the basso profundo of Barney Fife and the masculine articulations of Harvey Fierstein—that was my voice.

So I decided not to have a southern accent. I didn't want to be one of "them," with "them" defined as pretty much every human being I knew at that time. Part of this anger was teen angst, and part of it came from the fact that I actually was, and am, an obnoxious ass, but there was an earnest, legitimate longing, too. It wasn't just that I wanted to leave the South. I also had a vision of being a part of something else.

Where I really wanted to go, the home I was truly seeking—even if I never said it out loud—was a place I had heard about all my life. The North.

There are those who say "the North" is just a direction, while "the South" is a place. They're wrong. The North exists in a true and powerful way, and I know it does because we Southerners invented it.

The people I grew up with and live with today talk of it constantly. I don't know if it's got a precise longitude or latitude, but the North certainly exists, if only in the imaginations of suspicious Southerners.

For the devoted, fundamentalist Southerner, the North is any place that isn't the South. New York, Chicago, Seattle, these places are obviously part of the North, but so are San Diego, Tucson, and Santa Fe. Ask any Southerner and he'll tell you Washington, D.C., is part of the North. We do so for the same reason Northerners say D.C. is part of the South: We don't want it, either.

But the North I grew up with in my mind was the place where John Irving and Woody Allen lived. It wasn't just where Woody lived, it was where people lived who went to see his movies . . . and *liked* them. It was a place where a young man stretched askew across the sofa with a book was never asked, "Whatcha readin' that for?"

It was a place where people watched baseball, not football, because baseball was more artful, more intelligent, and less violent. Where a black man and a white woman who sat down in a restaurant together weren't stared at, or worse.

And for an angry, embattled, out-of-place teenager trapped in a backwood bastion of Old South bigotry and dim-wittery, the North that called to me was a powerful, compelling place that existed specifically to be not the South.

This is true North. You find references to this North in our most sacred southern texts: T-shirts and bumper stickers. No philosophy is held by the southern mind that can't be expressed in an 8" x 3" rectangle on the back of a truck, with room left over for the Confederate flag:

IF THE NORTH IS SO GREAT, WHY DON'T YOU GO BACK? or KEEP THE SOUTH CLEAN: BUY A YANKEE A BUS TICKET. And then there's the ever-popular WE DON'T CARE *HOW* YOU DID IT UP NORTH.

This is demonstrably untrue. We Southerners don't just care about how you do things up North, we're obsessed with it. We are painfully self-conscious of our relationship to the North. In part, we resent the snobbery and un-earned superiority we sometimes encounter. We are very aware that you think you're smarter, quicker, and more cosmopolitan than we are.

But what's worse—and this is the real source of fric-tion—we often suspect you are right. We just won't admit it. If he were being honest, the typical Southerner's bumper would read: EVEN IF WE UNDERSTOOD, WE *STILL* WOULDN'T CARE HOW YOU DID IT UP NORTH, or IF YOU'RE SO SMART, WHY ARE YOU HERE?

Southern scholars like C. Vann Woodward insist that this southern inferiority complex is rooted in the fact that (if you ignore that Vietnam thing) we're the only Ameri-cans to lose a war. Not me. I trace the southern ethos and its struggle against Northernism to the civil rights battle of the 1950s and '60s.

Let's turn again to the example of Senator Lieberman, who in 2000 bravely traveled across the South (those parts directly between Connecticut and Miami, anyway) as a lib-eral, Democratic, somewhat observant Jew. Despite the predictions and hand-wringing before the campaign, there were in fact no more cross burnings or synagogue bomb-ings or yarmulke snatchings in Macon, Georgia, than in Minneapolis-St. Paul.

Nevertheless, Senator Lieberman's southern campaign was instructive. It offered some interesting symbolism for the astute observer of history, for this wasn't Joe Lieberman's first tour of the old Confederacy He made another important trip in 1963, during the Civil Rights Movement.

According to the *New York Times,* "Mr. Lieberman was among 67 Yalies who formed the first large group of Northern white students to travel south for the cause of civil rights." Lieberman also participated in the 1963 March on Washington, where Martin Luther King, Jr., shared his dream with America.

One of the things I like about Joe Lieberman is that he hasn't attempted to exploit his youthful stand for civil rights. "I'm very proud that I went. It was a very important experience in my life. But, you know, there were others who were there much longer and did much more than I did," Lieberman told the *Times.*

His efforts were modest and, to his credit, so is he. It wasn't until Al Gore and Donna Brazille—the Slobodan Milosevic of the Democratic Party—revamped his résumé that Lieberman was offered to voters as the Harriet Tubman of the 2000 election.

Lieberman and the thousands of other Northerners, black and white, deserve credit for traveling to the Jim Crow South, and for all the right reasons. They didn't go there to learn from it or study it, but to defeat it. These "outside agitators" were waging a war against the southern culture of the time, and rightfully so.

What these civil rights warriors brought with them wasn't just a specific view of social justice or the rule of law. They brought a philosophy: Northernism. They saw up close the evils of racism, cronyism, anti-intellectualism, irrational religiosity, and general bad taste. They heard Southerners make claims of ethnic exceptionalism, arguing that what appeared unfair or irrational up North made perfect sense down home, and rejected them. These civil rights volunteers fought repeatedly against legal restrictions on the freedom to speak and to dissent. They would eventually support the creation of a federal television and radio network, in part to bring something resembling culture and enlightened entertainment to the region H. L. Mencken immortalized as "the Sahara of the Bozart."

We Southerners fought back—hard. We defended our traditions of racism, irrationality, and good-ol'-boy opportunity. We fought to keep things bad, and the Northernists (including some white Southerners) were pushing for changes to make things good. That's how it seemed to me as I grew up in the immediate aftermath of the civil rights struggle.

From my vantage point, Northernism represented meritocracy, the celebration of individual ability and achievement over race, class, and family connections. It represented culture, people who listened to jazz and attended operas without the word "Ol'" in the title. Northernism held high the standard of reason and demanded that all traditions and superstitions and heartfelt prejudices be measured by that standard.

These are broad generalizations, and many Southerners will no doubt scramble through their recollections of the Jim Crow South for the contrary example. But the fact that we can see and articulate this culture clash is proof that the two cultures, North and South, exist. And thanks to the efforts of people like Joe Lieberman and millions of others, the America of the 1960s and '70s was as northern as at any point in my lifetime. Southernism as an idea and practice had been defeated, dismissed, and discarded.

And today, watching and listening to one of those advocates of Northernism—now a U.S. senator from the state of Connecticut—championing the ideas of the modern, twenty-first-century American liberalism, the question immediately comes to mind: What happened to the real Joe Lieberman, and is the man on my TV set a pod person from another planet?

Virtually every idea he came to the South to fight in 1963, Joe Lieberman now champions forty years later. The old Joe Lieberman and his liberal friends fought against racial segregation in public schools. Today, those same liberals support race-based school admissions in places like California and Massachusetts that keep black children out of public schools because of their skin color.

The old Joe Lieberman opposed restrictions on free speech and fought against attempts by southern communities to squelch or suppress public debate. Today, northern liberals support restrictions on campaign ads under so-called campaign finance reform, and their children are the first people on liberal campuses to burn school newspapers for printing unpopular opinions.

The old Joe Lieberman reviled the claims of Southerners who said that their Confederate heritage and traditions could not be judged by northern standards. It was wrong to call southern institutions good or bad, Southerners argued, they were just different. Today, those same northern liberals promote multiculturalism, the belief that no culture—not even the barbaric culture of Islamic fundamentalism—can be judged by the West. There are no good or bad cultures, just different ones.

As for politics, much has been made of the infamous red/blue map of America in the 2000 presidential election between George W. Bush (a Southerner born in Milton,

Massachusetts) and Al Gore (a Yankee from Carthage, Tennessee). George W. Bush won a massive victory over Al Gore when measured by square miles but lost the popular vote by 500,000 or so.

But to see the North versus South cultural divide, ask yourself this question: Which presidential candidate in 2000 ran a campaign most reminiscent of old-style southern politics? Was it the campaign appealing to voters based on their race or religion? Was it the candidate who ran on a strategy of targeting uninformed voters through churches and bringing them into the polls to cast ballots based on instructions from the pulpit? The candidate who largely rejected intellectual appeals based on political principles and instead tried to connect with voters by using superficial shows of emotion and the good old-fashioned southern technique of pork barrel "What's In It For Me?" campaigning? Was this the true candidate of the South?

No, I'm not talking about George W. Bush. This race-based, lowest-common-denominator campaign was inflicted on America by Al Gore.

Gore ran a quintessentially southern campaign for president: race-based politics, antirational populism, playing the religion card (albeit from the kosher end of the deck) with his choice of Lieberman—who did everything but serve seder at his campaign events. Everything about Al Gore's presidential campaign was southern because all the essential ideas of America are the ideas of the Old South.

The only reason Gore and Lieberman lost the election was that they weren't quite southern enough: In a national election that was, essentially, a tie, George W. Bush beat

Al Gore in the thirteen states of the old Confederacy by 3.5 million votes. That's a larger margin than Ronald Reagan's *entire* margin over Jimmy Carter in 1980.

The Joe Lieberman generation supported government-funded radio and television to bring quality programming and access to fine arts to Southerners still enamored of drag racing and cockfights. Today, the children of the Civil Rights Movement from Boston to San Francisco Bay have made NASCAR America's number one spectator sport and spend their evenings glued to TV shows featuring has-been celebrities beating each other up and shame-free citizens wolfing down unmentionable pig parts for fun and profit.

In other words, the northern idealists of the 1960s like Joe Lieberman who once envisioned an American melting pot of opportunity, meritocracy, rationalism, antiracism (in theory, at least), progressivism, and individual enlightenment have devolved into acolytes of the United States of the Confederacy—a country of race-obsessed, ethnic clans dedicated to the proposition that it's not what you know but who you know; a society where intellectualism, if not actually feared, is looked upon as suspect; where superstition has so trumped reason that popular TV shows feature "psychics" talking to the dead victims of the September 11 terrorist attacks; where baseball—once the most popular sport of the American masses—is now considered "too intellectual." Instead, the modern American sports fan ensures that eight of the top ten most popular cable TV shows each week involve grown men wearing masks and hitting each other with folding chairs.

America, the Redneck Nation.

2

How the South Really Won the War

When I say the South "won the war," I don't mean *the* war. The defeat of the Confederacy was total. In fact, the Civil War was a classically southern enterprise: A handful of clods—without an army or a navy—come up with the lousy idea of starting a war, and their fellow Southerners are too polite to tell them how stupid they are. After attacking Fort Sumter, the South proceeds to get its butt kicked from Appomattox to Yazoo City, then announces, "We never wanted slavery, anyway," and blames the whole thing on the Yankees.

Before 1860, the South was one of the most wealthy and influential regions of America. From 1789 until 1856, nine of our nation's fourteen presidents were Southerners. America wouldn't elect another Southerner president until JFK was assassinated and Texan Lyndon Johnson was able to run as an incumbent in 1964.*

*Although Woodrow Wilson was born in Virginia and lived in (among other places) Columbia, South Carolina, no true Southerner can count the former president of Princeton and governor of New Jersey as a "Southern" president.

After 1865, the South was a destitute backwater on the verge of collapse. The wealthiest state in the Union— South Carolina—became the poorest. The southern intelligentsia, such as it was, was decimated or discredited. The blended Euro-Caribbean culture that was so alluring to nouveaux riches Northerners collapsed with the slave economy that maintained it.

The devastation was so thorough that sixty years later, H. L. Mencken wrote his classic commentary *Bozart of the South*, which noted the painfully obvious truth about the American South of the first half of the twentieth century: "In all that gargantuan paradise of the fourth-rate, there is not a single picture gallery worth going into, or a single orchestra capable of playing the nine symphonies of Beethoven, or a single opera-house, or a single theater devoted to decent plays." Most southern poetry and prose was drivel, he charged, and "when you come to critics, musical composers, painters, sculptors, architects and the like, you will have to give it up, for there is not even a bad one between the Potomac mud-flats and the Gulf." Nor, Mencken added, a historian, sociologist, philosopher, theologian, or scientist.

This was not a culture on the verge of national domination. Southern culture was on life support, full of poor white trash and even poorer scrabble-road blacks and a handful of self-declared gentry whose family wealth couldn't have bought them a midsize department store in Pittsburgh. Fifty years ago, telling people you were a Southerner was tantamount to telling people you were a failure, an oddball, or a rube.

Then came the 1960s and the American struggle for civil rights, a fight that most of us assume the South lost.

Outside agitators, thoughtful white Southerners, and determined black Southerners applied so much pressure that the Jim Crow era finally collapsed on itself. The laws changed. The lunch counters desegregated, as did the schools and office buildings—though the communities themselves did not.

For contemporary Southerners, the struggle of the 1960s was the battle that defined North and South. The 1960s were when the Confederate flag left the Klan rallies and climbed atop state capitols, when southern instincts were hardened into ideology, and when the stereotypes, North and South, solidified.

But the fundamental ideas of the South have become the fundamental ideas of America. The ideas that northern progressives went South to fight are now the enervating ideas of America. This is the war the South won.

I challenge you to name one significant idea the southern states fought to maintain in the Civil Rights Movement that has not become part of the American fabric.

The most obvious example is the most fundamental: racism. What is the core philosophy of all social life in the South? It's the idea that race matters, that race is determinant, that race is important, that your neighbors, your employers, and your government should treat people differently based on race.

This used to be called Jim Crow. Today, its name is Uncle Sam. It's hard to imagine a nation more obsessed with race and ethnicity than our own. Listen in on a meeting of state legislators in New York or a group of liberal city councilpersons in Wisconsin and it sounds like a beerhall putsch of Balkan warlords, dividing the spoils between the tribes.

When I was hosting a talk radio show in Charlotte, North Carolina, the local superintendent of schools attacked me publicly after I pointed out that the magnet school program he supported denied children admittance based on their race. There were approximately five hundred empty desks scattered across the district, but the thousand or more children applying were the wrong color—the magnet programs they wanted were already "too white" or "too black" to accommodate them.

"This is the same system used in schools all across the Northeast," he insisted on WBT one day. "How could it be racist?"

Exactly. Does anyone believe that Martin Luther King, Jr., was marching across the South to ensure that one day a black child would be kept out of a science class because there were already too many black kids in it? Sorting children in public schools based on their race was once viewed as the archetypal southern idea.

Today, it is the American one.

But the racism example is too easy, too obvious. The southern idea of race relations—that "race matters"—has clearly defeated the northern notion that it shouldn't. When Jesse Jackson, Kweisi Mfume, David Duke, Pat Buchanan, and the president of Harvard College all agree on something, we have clearly reached a national consensus.

So let's roll down the list. Merit? Anyone for the old northern notion of meritocracy?

As a front-of-the-class, hand-raising bookworm, the idea of merit as a fundamental value to be celebrated is near and dear to my heart. Anyone from "off" who has moved into a small southern town has felt the Stepford wives' sense of being out of place. There you can find lots of people with lots of the same last names working in the same place despite what appears to be a complete lack of competence.

As a young man, I knew that half the people working in my rural public school were incompetent cousins of well-placed politicos and midlevel district employees. I lived in the South. I expected it. But if you had told me that 57 percent of the incoming teachers in the Massachusetts public school system failed an eleventh-grade-level general knowledge test—and the state's solution was to *make the test easier*—then I would have been surprised. Well, guess what happened in Massachusetts in 1999 . . .

We're a nation of people-persons, completely dependent on networking to overcome incompetence. We're a total "Who's your daddy?" society where carpetbagging political novices with names like "Kennedy" and "Clinton" are regularly elected by "elitist" Northeasterners to high public offices, while voters on the West Coast give their support to clueless celebrities without a hint of shame.

Merit? Accomplishment? From the progressive income tax to the minimum wage, we insist that people who excel be punished for their efforts and those who fail be spared the consequences of their actions. From union-dominated public services to a limp-wristed criminal justice system, we are a nation dedicated to the Old South proposition that it's always somebody else's fault—especially if it's someone we already don't like.

And if Northernism is the celebration of intelligence and enlightenment, then the Land of Cotton must reach all the way to Saskatchewan. The current generation of Americans is the stupidest collection of humanoid life-forms to inhabit this continent since the first hunter-gatherers crossed the Bering Strait.

From the idiocy of the (mostly Yankee) voters in the 2000 election debacle to the popularity of the *Survivor* TV series to the utter informational vacuum in which the typical American lives, the ignorance I fled in my youth has infected our entire nation. In America today, stupidity is no longer a social ill. It's a lifestyle choice. I would call it an "alternative" lifestyle, but that would be like ACT-UP describing heterosexuality as the "alternative."

If you disagree, consider these facts:

According to the most recent National Adult Literacy Survey, between 40 million and 44 million Americans are unable to read phone books, ballots, car manuals, nursery rhymes, the Declaration of Independence, the Bible, the Constitution, or the directions on a medicine bottle. Another 50 million Americans recognize so few printed words that they are limited to a fourth- or fifth-grade level of reading and, therefore, have all subscribed to *USA Today*.

Further survey data reveal that 42 million Americans are able to perform only the simplest mathematical operations, like adding together two multidigit numbers. Forget the infamous butterfly ballot—you could confuse the typical American with a pair of dice.

Now, I ask you, is the idea of undisturbed ignorance a fundamentally northern or southern idea? I'm not saying there haven't always been idiots up North—Patrick Kennedy and Barbra Streisand are your problems, not ours. What I am saying is that I always thought that Northerners had the good sense to think they *ought* to be moderately intelligent and informed, while my fellow

Southerners' solution to meeting people with more information was to beat it out of them with a tire iron.

But from coast to coast, the idea of pursuing knowledge for knowledge's sake is more suspect than ever. It's no coincidence that there are virtually no world-class universities south of Charlottesville, Virginia, but the South has led the way on state-sponsored vocational and technical education. You can drive from New Orleans to Norfolk and not pass a single state-run institution that can compete with the typical northeastern prep school, but if your car breaks down on the trip, there'll be ten mechanics with tech diplomas before you can get the hood up.

Why? Because Southerners have largely rejected the idea of abstract intellectualism, a.k.a. "book learnin'." Or, in the words of my uncle Teenyboy, "Boy, you got plenty of book learnin', but you ain't got the sense God gave a pissant!"

The idea of "book learnin'" is that the kind of information you get from an active intellectual life is somehow suspect, is of less value than *real* learning, which is what you get from the hands-on experience of working on machines, planting crops, stump-breaking cattle, etc. What can you possibly learn from any book (except the Bible, of course) that's really worth knowing, unless it's got photos of a car or a woman's titties? If it's got both, you don't read it: You hang it on the wall of your shop.

In the 1960s, the most popular college kids majored in the abstract fields of history, political science, or the arts, hoping to expand their minds, explore the mysteries of existence, and get laid. Today, our most elite college campuses are covered over in pre-law and business majors because the students feel the need to be utilitarian. They, too, fear the label "book learnin'" and instead want to show how their education will pay the bills. From Harvard to Stanford, everybody's in tech school.

And then there's sex, a topic that, as a man who's been married for more than a decade, I can only write about from rumor and vague recollection.

The hallmark of southern sexuality has always been its intemperateness. The paragons of southern women were Flora and Fauna. Flora, the delicate southern flower whose gentility was ever guarded by her daddy, her Bible, or her Smith & Wesson; and Fauna, the tattooed trailer tramp who knew seventeen home cures for the clap but not the name of the guy passed out on her sofa. The southern women I panted after in my youth were either nuts or sluts. If they weren't praying to Jesus to send them a husband in the next shipment of touring gospel singers, they were on the pool table under a pile of fraternity brothers. I couldn't seem to connect with women who were able to maintain a grown-up relationship based on engaging ideas, intellectual curiosity, mutual respect, and the occasional use of handcuffs.

What I wanted, I always thought, was a New York romance, the kind I saw in Woody Allen movies: intelligent, sexual people whose psychoses were fascinating but whose behavior didn't fall into boorishness. Of course, that was before Mr. Allen—the ultimate Yankee—went southern and started screwing his children.

And have you seen HBO's *Sex and the City*? What is this show except for a collection of well-coiffed trailer trash moved to Manhattan? What amazes me about this show isn't the shocking sexual content, it's that I knew of redneck women engaged in all these bizarre, self-destructive behaviors twenty years ago! Who knew that America's model for modern womanhood would be the

Tammy Faye look-alike I heard about in high school who had to be rescued from her mobile home after she got a household appliance irretrievably lodged in her nether regions?

Every day, in every way, my country is getting more and more redneck. All through high school, I dreamed of getting away from a society where stupidity was celebrated, where achievement was resented, where intelligence was suspect, and where the best way to spend time without taking your pants off was watchin' NASCAR.

Today, I find myself surrounded by the cast of a Ferrely Brothers movie, waiting in line for an ill-educated dolt to screw up my next consumer transaction in a country where, according to the *Wall Street Journal,* the number one most watched sport is now . . . NASCAR!

I can't buy a break.

It is simply beyond debate that America is today a more southern nation than it has been at any time since the Civil War. Those of you who are resisting this obvious truth are doing so by hiding behind the thin reed of exceptionalism. You know some smart Southerner or some dumb Northerner or you saw Spike Lee's *Do the Right Thing* and its overt racist stupidity or you had the most moving moment of your life at a homosexual marriage of a mixed-race couple at an interdenominational church in Muscle Shoals, Alabama.

And, of course, you're right that these exceptions exist. That's my point. They stand out for being exceptional. They don't fit the norm of North and South that you and I both recognize.

The insipid ideas that southern whites fought for during the civil rights struggle—that it's okay to stay stupid, that it's easier to blame those who point out that you're wrong than it is to figure out how to do what's right, and, of course, the right to treat people differently based on race—these ideas have overwhelmed by force the principles of merit, intelligence, self-criticism, and antiracism that the North once stood for. We are truly one nation, one giant Redneck Nation.

I wanted out of the South because it was obsessed with race and ethnic identity, so I went to New York—where a city councilwoman was almost forced to resign after making a joke about Irish people drinking beer on St. Patrick's Day. The punch line: The woman was Irish.

I was tired of always being asked, "Who's your daddy?" I wanted to go someplace where merit counted for more than who you know. So I went to Chicago, a city run *entirely* on a "who you know" system, down to getting a garbage can from your local alderman

The irrational fervor of southern evangelicalism drove me into the camp of the Infidels, so I went to California and hung out with crystal-wearing vegan spiritualists, one of whom (I swear it's true) told me her cat could say "mommy."

I thought if I heard Charlie Daniels yowling another redneck anthem about killing all the foreigners, I would join the French foreign legion and volunteer to invade Nashville. So I went to Omaha and watched men spit artful designs of brown tobacco juice out the window of their pickup trucks while sitting at a stoplight.

Journalists like Peter Applebaum who write that the South is becoming ever more like the rest of America have it completely backward. They see Sun Belt growth, snowbird migration, and New South sprawl and conclude that population growth and immigration are making a South that is "more like America."

Wrong. It's America that is ever more like the South. I'm not talking about the political trends: southern presidents, Senate leaders, and Speakers of the House. That's not about culture—that's demographics.

Does it ever occur to anyone why, if entire boroughs of New York are emigrating southward, the South has gotten more Republican and conservative in the past ten years? Why not the opposite? Why aren't northern Democrats turning the tide in the South, at least in places like Florida, which, as of this writing, has a GOP governor and state legislature?

It's because the folks from Jersey and Ohio were already rednecks when they got here. By that I mean that they already held the essential southern principles of race, irrationality, fear of merit, and a love for the insipid.

That's what I mean by Redneck Nation. I'm not arguing that America is turning into a nation of banjo pickers and cousin kissers. I'm not saying that the U.S. is suddenly ready to sing "Dixie" or convert en masse to mustard-based barbecue.

What I see—and what seems to be undeniably true—is that the fundamental ideas of the South forty years ago are now the fundamental ideas of America. It's as if the Freedom Riders of the 1960s were all infected by trichinosis and Dixietosis and went back to Minneapolis and Manhattan, inadvertently spreading an epidemic.

Those beer-bellied rednecks have been telling me all my life that the South was gonna do it again, and I'll be damned if they weren't right. The South did win the war. But Americans are just too dumb to know it.

3

Where Is the South?

When I was covering the 2000 presidential election for *National Review Online,* I wrote: "The only state south of Iowa Dukakis won was the Democratic stronghold of West Virginia—a state no true Southerner will claim."

This was a mistake.

One offhand comment inspired a torrent of indignant responses. West-by-God-Virginians wrote to insist that they were members in good standing of the Confederacy. Haughty Virginians asserted just as strongly that their cousins from the mountains are Yankee turncoats.

"Someone should tell Michael Graham that West Virginia's most famous son, Stonewall Jackson, was from West Virginia," wrote one southern loyalist from the land of Senator Robert Byrd.

Oh, yeah? "I'm sure General Stonewall would prefer to say he was from western Virginia, since the state of West Virginia wasn't created by the Yankees until after his death," was one Virginian's reply.

For Southerners, as for the Good Lord, a thousand years is but the blink of an eye.

So where is the South? In their definitive work *1001 Things Everyone Should Know About the South,* John Shelton Reed and Dale Volberg Reed offer several definitions:

- Below the Mason-Dixon line, which is essentially the Maryland-Pennsylvania border
- The official Bureau of the Census definition, which includes Maryland, Delaware, and Oklahoma, but not Missouri (confirming for people everywhere that the federal government is, in fact, run by morons)
- The states of the old Confederacy, a definition that overlooks the Civil War schizophrenia of Missouri, Kentucky, and the Oklahoma territory

But as any Southerner will tell you, maps don't mean grits when it comes to where the South really is. Indeed, John Shelton Reed argues that a state is southern if the people who live there think it is. For example, Oklahomans consistently tell pollsters that they are southern and their communities are in the South, even though the typical cowboy wouldn't know a mint julep if you poured it over his Stetson.

Or take the peculiar case of the once and perhaps future presidential candidate Al Gore, who repeatedly claimed to be a "true son of the South," which reinforced the Southerners' belief that everyone from Washington, D.C., is a liar.

Despite its location on the Potomac, few Southerners today claim the nation's capital. John Shelton Reed notes that, before World War II, Washington had the society and spirit (and segregation) of a traditional southern city. It has since become a "company town for the federal government," and given the South's contrarian relationship with the national government since, well, 1860, D.C. is now solidly enveloped by the great Yankee Empire.

Not surprisingly, Al Gore did very well in D.C.

But does anyone in America even acknowledge the North/South boundary anymore? Does geography or regionalism even matter? The idea is often dismissed by academics and political observers who see a bland and blanched America. They are wrong.

For those who insist that we live in a homogenized, supersized America whose significant regional differences have been washed away beneath a tidal wave of Coca-Cola and cable TV, I offer the following from Northerner Mark Strauss:

> Imagine then, for just a moment, the North as its own nation. Trent Lott and Dick Armey would be foreigners. We would no longer be subjected to round-the-clock TV commercials for Dale Earnhardt commemorative plates. [A] new liberal majority would be able to pass tougher gun laws and legislation barring discrimination against gays and lesbians. . . . We could implement "Plan South Carolina" to convince tobacco growers to develop alternative crops. Northern observers could ensure democracy in Florida polling places. Peace Corps volunteers could teach . . . Southerners to pull themselves out of poverty and illiteracy while simultaneously promoting a better understanding of American values.

When these words appeared in *Slate.com*, Mark Strauss
was senior editor at the prestigious but unread *Foreign
Policy* magazine. His essay, "Let's Ditch Dixie: The Case
for Northern Secession," made the funny, satirical, and
painfully truthful argument that the economic, cultural,
and political standing of America's northern states would
be immediately improved if Southerners were granted the
independence we fought for in 1861. Should we Southerners be so ungracious as to decline this belated but
generous offer of reverse secession, Strauss recommends
that his fellow Yankees give us the boot. Among Mr.
Strauss's more compelling facts:

- More people live below the poverty line in the old
  Confederacy than in all of the Northeast and Midwest combined.
- You are three times more likely to be murdered in
  parts of Dixie than anywhere in New England.
- The South has the highest infant-mortality rate, the
  highest incidences of sexually transmitted diseases,
  and the lowest SAT scores.
- The Confederate states rail against the tyranny of big
  government, yet they are the largest recipients of
  federal tax dollars.

Mr. Strauss's facts were straight, his logic impeccable, and
his humor dead-on:

Economically and socially, secession will be pain-
less for the North. The South is a gangrenous limb
that should have been lopped off decades ago.
They steal business away from the North the same

way that developing countries worldwide have always attracted foreign direct investment: through
low wages and anti-union laws. The flow of guns
into America's Northern cities stems largely from
Southern states. The tobacco grown by ol' Dixie
kills nearly a half-million Americans each year.

In fact, the only obvious downside is that the
South would almost certainly insist on keeping the
3,150 nuclear warheads that are scattered throughout Georgia, Texas, Louisiana, and Virginia. Maybe
we could strike a deal to get those nukes back, the
same way Russia did with Ukraine after the Soviet
Union broke up. If not, then perhaps national mis-
sile defense might not be such a bad idea after all.

I enjoyed the article so much that I called Mr. Strauss's office to arrange an interview, but I barely got the request
out before his assistant on the other end of the phone
shut me down.

"Mr. Strauss has no further comment on this topic. His
article was intended as satire." *Click.*

Strauss's assistant had hung up on me. For a moment
I thought, "Great, another rude New Yorker." But something in the tone of the beleaguered voice at the other
end of the line sounded . . . familiar. I jumped on the In-
ternet, checked a few Confederista websites, and, just as
I suspected, Mark Strauss was under siege, pinned down
by incoming fire from the last soldiers of the Lost Cause.

Southern partisans were outraged by Strauss's comments and thrilled that a Yankee had finally admitted what
Southerners long suspected: Y'all want to get rid of us at
the first opportunity. So the tireless, obsessed Confederate-

flag wavers who make up the Confederacy of Dunces were letting Strauss have it with both barrels.

Is there any man more pathetic than the Southerner still defending the Confederacy? The Confederista spends his days calling radio talk shows, arguing that the "War of Northern Aggression" had nothing to do with slavery; he drifts to sleep each night dreaming of taking Washington after the Second Manassas; occasionally he can be found dressed in a hot, scratchy uniform of gray wool, bathing in the re-created glory of some minor victory snatched from a collective past dominated by crushing defeat.

Satire? Satire expended upon the contemporary male Confederate has the same effect as a sexual advance from another man: It's got to be pretty obvious for him to realize what's going on, and when he does, he's not likely to appreciate it.

What these baleful Southerners wish to return to, I cannot say. Who wants to go back to feudalism, where a handful of feudal lords prospered from the toil of the masses of poor, uneducated serfs?

Alas, the modern Confederistas are like California New Agers who believe in reincarnation: They were all Napoleons in a previous life.

One of America's most prominent Confederistas is Michael Hill, head whackjob at the loony League of the South—an obscure organization which has already declared southern cultural independence. After the Strauss piece was published, Hill jumped at the chance to defend his "southron" heritage. He promptly published a rebuttal claiming that all the benefit of secession would be accrued to the South: "A Southern nation composed of only the eleven States of the former Confederacy would have

74 million people, the thirteenth most populous in the world." Its economy, Hill noted, would be the world's fourth largest, behind the (newly shrunken) U.S. of A., Japan, and Germany.

"God willing, after [secession] we Southerners will be busy enjoying the sweet fruits of a free and prosperous republic," Professor Hill wrote, "founded on private property, free association, fair trade, sound money, low taxes, limited regulation of business, equal justice before the law, secure border, gun rights, protection of the unborn, and an absence of entangling foreign alliances. In other words, Mr. Strauss, we'll have a civilization and you will not."

It's just a suggestion, but somebody may want to double the guard at Fort Sumter.

What this tempest in an iced tea glass reveals is the strength of the idea of North and South, and the opposition of attitudes they represent. The South exists strongly enough for Northerners to mock it and Southerners to defend it. Its ideology is clear enough for Mark Strauss to fear it and Professor Hill to advance it as superior. The differentiation of the two cultures, North and South, is so apparent to all observers that they can be analyzed and debated.

And, as the great Southerner Fred Nietzsche observed, cultures cannot coexist. They collide. They struggle, they battle, until one has been vanquished and the other has triumphed. So we come back to the question: Who won? Which of these two cultures dominates America as a whole? Is Southernism limited to the lower right-hand corner of the map, or does the Confederate banner (or the ideas it represents, at least) fly from sea to shining sea?

To find out, let's take the Where Are You? quiz. Please answer each of the following questions with the word "North" or "South":

- You take your young son to enroll at the local public school. The principal refuses to enroll him because he's black. Where are you?
- You live in a place where 80 percent of your neighbors will read just one book (or less) this year. Where are you?
- You are outraged by an action taken by a Republican politician. You head to the copy shop, whip up some fliers denouncing the lout, and head to the local public park to pass them out. You're arrested by the sheriff, who tells you that your town doesn't allow any disruptive political speech in public. Where are you?
- You turn on your TV and the most popular show of the week is a boxing match between has-been sitcom celebrities. The number one CD at the music store features the illiterate rantings of gold-toothed wanna-be pimps looking for yet another word that rhymes with "bitch." Where are you?
- Your local newspaper reports that one-third of all the children in your area are born out of wedlock. But it won't matter, since 40 percent won't be able to read their own birth certificates. Where are you?

Since you're smart enough to be reading a book, you've figured out that all of these incidents come from the

North. More accurately, they apply to America as a whole. The stereotype of a racist, illiterate, well-censored collection of tasteless dopes has expanded beyond the confines of the Confederacy and encompasses the entire nation.

While there is a clear difference between Northernism and Southernism, there is no significant difference between America's North and South. Northern liberalism, in its modern form, is indistinguishable from the Old South ideology that Northerners fear and mock.

After reading the debate between Strauss and Hill, what is the real difference between the two sides? Yes, Dr. Hill is right that the South could exist as a separate nation, and yes, Mark Strauss is correct in noting that the per capita wealth, health, and intelligence of the remaining United States would increase immediately. But the supposedly conflicting sides actually represent nothing more than a balance of power between different applications of the same ideas.

The Confederistas would love to abandon the confines of the U.S. Constitution and the protection of individual liberties found therein. In fact, these liberties are viewed by Southerners as mere annoyances.

But with the exception of recently deceased Strom Thurmond and Jesse Helms (What? They're *not* dead? Check again, please!), who wants a resegregated South where the rights to assemble and speak are trumped by the majority's right to stomp "outside agitators"? Certainly not the 30 percent of the South's population that is non white, not to mention the one in seven Southerners born outside the South.

On the other hand, Mr. Strauss's argument for a South-free U.S.A. is just as repellent. In his vision of America, he celebrates the potential triumph of central government, of "a new liberal majority" that could get to work gutting the Second Amendment without a bunch of yay-hoos complainin' about it. We could end all this nonsense about the government having to compensate you for turning your private property into a protected habitat for the spotted snail darter. And we could finally pass some real hate-crime laws—you know, the kind that throw people into jail for expression of any non-state-approved opinion.

What smug Northerners like Mr. Strauss cannot see is that they are advocating the same fundamental principals as their southern counterparts. Northern liberals merely apply these principles from a different angle. Is Strauss saying that dumping the South would also let him dump the Second Amendment of the Constitution? How is that significantly different from his belief that evangelical Southerners are constantly trying to dump the First?

Would a Northern America adjust each citizen's legal status based on his skin color or whom he has sex with? Gee, the South was doing that for years until the North intervened.

Tired of those NASCAR ads on TV, Mark? You need to talk to the folks in New Hampshire and Chicago, where they are building racetracks as fast as they can.

And if it's southern illiteracy he fears, he should drop in on the public schools in Cleveland, Detroit, and Washington, D.C.—perhaps the worst in the nation. Good northern liberals are the most impassioned opponents of an educational voucher system that would let the children in these schools escape to the private sector tomorrow. Perhaps it's because, like the bigoted Southerners they look down on, they don't want their kids going to school with poor black kids, either.

In other words, the difference between Mr. Strauss's North and Dr. Hill's South is one of mere geography. Same ideas, applied from a different direction. And nearly all those are ideas happily supplied by the solid American South.

4

North vs. South: A Primer

In the South, white people hate black people and black people hate white people. In New York, it's the other way around.

• In the South, race is the single most important public issue in people's daily lives. In New York, ethnicity is the single most important issue. Which means, in South Carolina, people can hate each other on sight, but in New York, they have to wait until they've been properly introduced and know each other's last names.

• In New York, my support of the Second Amendment and opposition to legalized abortion made me a right-wing zealot. Down South, my support of free speech and opposition to the death penalty make me a commie.

• Southerners understand that the War Between the States was caused by many factors and that slavery was one of the complex issues that must be looked at in the political, economic, and social contexts of the time, which means it is difficult, if not impossible, to say what one issue caused the war. In New York, nobody cares who started the damn war. We won. You lost. Get over it.

- In New York, the fact that I used to go hunting—with an actual *gun*—made me a Neanderthal. In the South, the fact that I stopped makes me a homosexual.

- In New York, I was expected to be impressed by the local Italian cuisine, which was often one fistful of garlic away from Chef Boyardee. If I didn't say that a mediocre meal of shells and sauce was *molto bene* at least five times, my hosts were insulted.

- In South Carolina, people aren't expecting you to be impressed by the food, they just expect you to eat it. If I said, "Man, this is great," more than once over a plate of to-die-for chicken and mouthwatering homemade dumplings, my host would assume I was there to sell something.

- In New York, the assumption was that, in any conversation not involving frog gigging, any Southerner was the dumbest person at the table. If I was sitting in the backseat looking at a map and telling a New Yorker which Manhattan street to turn on, he would ignore me, take the wrong turn, then scream profanity at me because I got him lost.

- In the South, the assumption is that, in any conversation, we Southerners are the dumbest people at the table. That's why we don't want to hear how you do it up North. Thanks for the help, but we'd rather screw it up ourselves.

- New Yorkers pretend they've read books they haven't. Southerners deny reading the ones they have.

- Down South, it's impossible for a person to be too quiet. In New York, it's impossible to be too loud.

• In the South, you're a racist if you send your kids to an all-white private school instead of the integrated public one. In New York, you're a racist if you support vouchers, which would allow black kids to attend the same all-white private schools your kids do.

• In southern restaurants, there is no such thing as "too much." The same is true in New York, except it applies to the price.

• Southerners consider Woody Allen a sick, perverted weirdo who makes movies for New York Jews. In New York, nobody ever calls Woody a Jew, but they don't call him a pervert, either.

• Down South, a great Saturday means you never had to go inside. In New York, it means you never had to go out.

• In the South, locals tend to resent people they meet who are smarter than they are. In New York, locals never meet anybody who is.

• In New York, the Yankees can win back-to-back World Series, and the fans say, "Yeah, but whaddaya bums gonna do *this* year?" In South Carolina, the local college team can lose twenty-one straight games, and the fans say, "Yeah, but remember back in '89 when they almost had a shot at the national title?"

• In the South, it's okay for a kid to handle a gun, but giving him a condom might inspire inappropriate behavior. In New York, condoms are in middle-school vending machines, but dodgeball is banned from playgrounds for inspiring inappropriate behavior.

• In the South, a woman who stays home with her children while her husband works is called a hero. In New

York, a woman who stays home to raise children is called a nanny.

- In New York, the most commonly heard phrases at showings of foreign films are "He's no Fellini" and "It breathes with ironic pathos." Down South, the most commonly heard phrases are "Subtitles? What's that?" and "Baby, you ever bring me to another one a these readin' pictures, I'm gonna whup you."

5

Rednecks and White Whine

*The Southerner who is chiefly heard from is apparently all toes;
one cannot have commerce with him without stepping on them.
Thus he protests hysterically every time northern opinion is
intruded into his consideration of his problems, and northern
opinion, so often called to book, now prudently keeps out. The
result is that the Southerner struggles alone, and that he goes
steadily from bad to worse.*

—H.L. Mencken

Meet Fudgie, a symbol of our new All-Redneck Nation.

Fudgie, a fifty-two-year-old retired baker, is from Ohio,
not down South. He's a proud member of the Independent Bikers' Association, Cincinnati chapter. That's "biker"
as in Harley, not Schwinn; cycling is an archetypically
northern activity. In the South, real men don't ride anything that can't be floored, gunned, or whipped—which
may explain the condition of our women.

So how did Fudgie—a.k.a. Carl Campbell—come to
represent the newly southern America? It's not because he

rides a Harley, an honorable avocation on either side of the Mason-Dixon line. And it's not because he weighs more than three hundred pounds, though we Southerners do like a man with a figure. No, Fudgie and his biker buddies became true soldiers of the Confederacy when they bravely rode their hogs into the nearest courtroom and burst into tears.

The motorcycled members of Ohio's citizenry have officially claimed victim status. They are beset by antibiker discrimination, they claim. Restaurants shun them, bars ban them, and pedestrians fear them. And, the bikers say, it's starting to hurt their feelings.

According to the *New York Times,* Ohio's motorcycle enthusiasts feel that their rights as citizens have been trampled upon. So these delicate flowers, still stinging from being made unwelcome by the maître d' at the Four Seasons, asked State Representative Sylvester Patton of Youngstown to sponsor a bill levying a five-hundred-dollar civil fine against any business found guilty of discriminating against people "because they operate motorcycles or wear clothing that displays the name of a motorcycle-related organization or group."

The same cycle riders who oppose Big Brother's efforts to force them to wear helmets want that same government to force restaurants and hotels not to notice when they wear those helmets into the building.

How big a problem could this alleged antibiker discrimination be? It's hard to imagine the shop owner or tavern keeper willing to walk up to a three-hundred-pound leather-clad biker with "Born to Violate the Laws of Nature" tattooed across his biceps and say, "We don't serve your kind around here." It's even harder to imagine

Fudgie as a victim of, well, just about anything, except maybe a massive coronary.

At the risk of offending Fudgie's delicate sensibilities, might I point out that one way to prevent business owners from treating you like a thug is to stop dressing like one? If a guy walks into a restaurant wearing a pillowcase with eye-holes and carrying a rope with a slipknot, he really shouldn't complain if some folks don't want to sit in his section.

There's also the wimp factor. When did bikers become babies? I expect tough guys on Harleys to display a quiet stoicism, not to go running to the state legislature crying, "A big bully just made fun of my nose ring!"

But that's precisely what bikers have done. They have staked their claim on the American gold mine of victim-hood. And in a nation mesmerized by the gratifying self-righteousness and soothing powerlessness that come with victimhood, the exemplar of this whiny, complaining, eas-ily insulted, put-upon, sore-toed groaner is the southern white male.

Before there was the NAACP or GLAAD or NAAFA (the National Association for the Advancement of Fat Accep-tance), there were rednecks. As Mencken noted, they are a notoriously thin-skinned bunch.

Southern white males have a long tradition of kvetching Confederate-style. The first Europeans reached Charleston, South Carolina, in 1670 and promptly began whining that Plymouth Rock was getting all the attention. Southerners proceeded to pout their way through the entire Revolu-tionary War. The South was a hotbed of Toryism, the locals constantly attempting to make deals with the British and blaming the entire mess on the Yankees in Massachusetts.

After holding the Constitution hostage over the issue of

slavery in the 1780s, Southerners spent the next 170 years complaining about being picked on over the issue. Listening to slave owners and their political allies of the day, you'd think *they* were the victims of the slave economy: "Slaves are expensive, they eat so much, they keep trying to run away (those ungrateful bastards), and the only reason we have them is that Northerners force us to keep selling cotton for huge profits. It's all their fault."

So the South started a war and then complained because the Yankees fought back. They established Jim Crow segregation, then whined when blacks rose up to protest it. They created a two-tiered education system designed to lower education standards for working-class citizens, then complained of anti-Southern bigotry whenever someone noted the South had the dumbest population in America.

During the Civil Rights Movement, Americans largely rejected this idiocy and sided with the real victims of southern racism. The rest of the country understood that white Southerners *felt* put-upon and out of sorts, but Northerners rejected these feelings as delusional. Americans of the 1950s and '60s, watching the prejudice and violence of the southern establishment, saw for themselves who the victims were and who they weren't. And America told the ever-whiny rednecks to stuff a sock in it.

In fact, I would argue that at a fundamental level, the Civil Rights Movement was a wholesale rejection of victim status as a good in itself. Young black southern men who sat down at lunch counters knowing they would soon be locked up and beaten down weren't whiny crybabies. They took their lumps and came back the next day. And this they did to generate anger, not pity.

Dr. King and his allies who marched toward the barking dogs and water cannons weren't worried about hurt feelings. They had concussions and contusions on their minds, but they kept marching. They weren't claiming victimhood, they were accepting consequences.

I can't see the people who suffered and fought back against Jim Crow as victims. To call them so would be, in my opinion, an insult. "Victim" implies helplessness, neediness, an inability to defend oneself. Black Southerners who challenged segregation were nothing of the sort. I would no more call Martin Luther King a victim than I would call Mother Teresa a pauper. It's demeaning and misses the point.

That's the impression the Civil Rights Movement left upon me. But something happened between Selma, Alabama, and the creation of the white man's Southern Anti-Defamation League today. Forty years after the Civil Rights Movement, being a victim isn't an insult, it's an honor. From the incompetent mom-'n'-pop shopkeeper on the corner (a "victim" of corporate interests like Wal-Mart) to the idiot spokespeople for various special-interest groups (even fat people have the aforementioned NAAFA, a lobbying organization opposed, one assumes, to gravity) to entire nationalities (the Serbs and Palestinians come to mind), everybody wants to be a victim—southern-style.

WHINY, HAPPY PEOPLE

America is now a nation where nothing is ever one's own fault. And, my northern brethren, you learned it from us. When the NAACP was boycotting South Carolina for flying the Confederate flag on the capitol dome, I used to mock my fellow South Carolinians for claiming they were "victims" of an unfair boycott. "C'mon, gang!" I told them. "For nearly a hundred years, that flag has flown over Klan rallies and civil rights counterdemonstrations. What's the NAACP supposed to do? Add it to their letterhead? It is our statehouse over which that flag flies, and it is our elected legislature that keeps it there against all reason and good counsel. Of course, we citizens are going to suffer. We're supposed to!"

Listening to thick-necked white guys whine about the "bullying tactics" of the NAACP was an absolute laugh. As young men, many of these same flag supporters over-turned school buses, blocked restaurant doors, and shouted "nigger" as the freedom marchers passed. Today, these same men, older but no wiser, wish us to believe that they are now the victims of a black power juggernaut.

So like I said, I used to make fun of these simpering Southerners constantly. Then, dear Yankee, I met you.

I met the aforementioned National Association for the Advancement of Fat Acceptance, a group so painfully fat-headed it has to be headquartered in California. NAAFA's position is that fat people should not be victimized by their excessive mass or high-calorie lifestyle. No, the rest of us should suffer for their obesity instead.

I must confess that I find it difficult to take the full-figured flaks at NAAFA seriously. The first time I heard the name of the organization, I thought it was some sort of agricultural advocacy group, like the Dairy Board or Beef Council. You know, with catchy slogans like "Fat: It Keeps a Body Warm!" or "The *Other* Other White Meat (or meat-like substance)."

According to NAAFA, fat folks are the victims of biology, genealogy, gastroenterology, and, for all I know, archaeology and Scientology, too. People are fat because they are oppressed by the evil diet industry, the evil pharmaceutical interests, and the What Are We Going to Do with All These Lime-Green Stretch Pants? cabal.

In other words, if it weren't for all the diet products, low-cal foods, and social emphasis on good looks and health, these people would be skin and bones by now. Instead, the spokesperson for the NAAFA I spoke with weighed 375 pounds, due entirely (she claimed) to failed diets and an insulin imbalance.

Claiming to be a victim because you spend your days flopped down in front of *General Hospital* with Dr Pepper, Colonel Sanders, and Little Debbie—yep, that's southern, all right. But seizing victim status while making everyone else suffer—that's redneck!

And so NAAFA and its allies have mounted a campaign to end the "discrimination" against obese people. You own a tanning salon and you refuse to hire Wanda the Whale to welcome your customers—you get sued. You own a health food store and don't think a four-hundred-pound employee fits into your marketing scheme—get a lawyer. And if your house catches fire in California and a ladder truck rolls up out front staffed with sumo wrestlers who can't climb the ladder—that's America's victim culture at work.

In the old, evil, bigoted days before NAAFA, a fire safety employee had to be able to do certain things, little things irrelevant to public safety like, oh, climb a fire truck ladder without breaking it. Some fire department employees were even expected to be able to climb up this ladder and back down again *while carrying another person.*

The problem is that when you're 5'10" and 350 pounds, you're already carrying the equivalent of another person around every day of your life. Three wouldn't just be a crowd, it would be a hernia.

These expectations of mobility and strength prevented some obese fire department applicants from being hired. Bigotry, oppression—and the old-fashioned belief that it's stupid to hire people for a job they are physically incapable of accomplishing—combined to deny these Super-Sized citizens their rights. So these husky would-be hose pullers went to court . . . and won. And thanks to a court ruling, obese people are no longer victims. Instead, the victims now are the taxpayers who have to pay the salaries of these rotund fire truck riders. The taxpayers must also pay normal-sized firefighters who are actually competent and able to do the lifesaving work.

Then there are the potential victims, the people in the burning buildings or emergency situations who cannot be served by these public safety employees.

An America infused with the values of self-reliance and objective justice as championed by the old Civil Rights Movement would laugh these lard-butted loons out of court. But in a truly southern America, these self-declared victims are as at home as a pig in slo . . . Uh, you know what I mean.

And only in a Redneck Nation dominated by "it's not my fault" Southernism could people who smoked three packs a day for thirty years have the nerve to appear before a jury and blame the cigarettes. In 2000, CNN reported that a San Francisco jury awarded $20 million to Leslie Whitcley, a forty-year-old smoker who admitted she never, ever smoked a cigarette that she didn't know could hurt her. How, how, *HOW* can a woman who has picked up a cigarette, put it in her mouth, set it on fire, and smoked it—then repeated the action fifty times a day, every single day, for twenty-seven years—how can that woman look at a jury and say, "But wait—it was an accident"?

This is a claim of victimhood that ranks up there with Bill Clinton blaming his pants problem on Ken Starr (true story) and former Symbionese Liberation Army bomber Kathleen Soliah claiming to be a victim of the 9/11 terrorist attacks (true and sickening story). You could only get away with this nonsense in a Redneck Nation.

Worse than the "victims" of the right to smoke are the Smoke Nazis who dream of living in a world where we have no rights at all.

Across the Great Northern America, liberal communities like Los Angeles and Montgomery County, Maryland, have banned smoking outdoors at public parks. Why? To protect the "victims" of secondhand smoke, of course. Only one problem: When it comes to smoking outdoors, there *are* no victims of secondhand smoke. Outdoor smoking may annoy you, but not even the most extreme Smoke Nazi has presented evidence that the dangers of secondhand smoke extend into the ionosphere.

Not to be outdone, in 2001, the same Montgomery County (an enclave of northern-style liberalism) passed an ordinance that would have essentially banned smoking in the privacy of your own home. Under this new county regulation, if you were sitting in front of the TV having a cigarette and your neighbor could even smell it, he could call the county EPA and you would be exposed to a fine of up to $750.

After a bombardment of international mockery, this ludicrous law was laughed into oblivion. When folks asked how any legislative body could criminalize smoking in one's own home, an angry Montgomery County council-man insisted the law was perfectly reasonable: "This does not say that you cannot smoke in your house. What it does say is that your smoke cannot cross property lines."

In other words, oxygen tents make good neighbors.

Now, I know that if I smoke enough cigarettes, they could kill me. And I know that if someone locked you and me together in an unventilated room, my smoke might—I repeat, *might*—kill you. But nobody has ever demonstrated that if I wrap myself in Red Man chewing tobacco, sit down in my fireplace, and set myself ablaze, it's going to give you so much as a mild cough in your house across the street.

Who is the victim of a smoker lighting up in his own living room? Whom are the self-righteous Smoke Nazis protecting this time? Aha! This is where the southern victim value system really kicks in. In the world of rednecks, you don't have to prove you're a victim. You simply declare yourself one, and the wheels of the world grind to a halt.

What a warped sense of justice we have when the working stiff sitting on his sofa watching *All in the Family* and smoking a Lucky is the oppressor, and the paranoiac upstairs sniffing the air vents and calling the cops is the victim.

And if the guy upstairs feels victimized by my neighbor's cigarettes, wait until he smells my Macanudo. Or my mother's corned beef and cabbage. Or me, after *eating* my mom's corned beef and cabbage . . .

Then there's my dad's cheap aftershave, my baby's poopy diaper, and my dog's various odiferous events. (I don't actually have a dog, but I could get one if you keep calling the cigarette cops, you jerk.)

All of this, inspired by hypersensitive simps who never once had to demonstrate that, by reasonable standards, they had been victimized in any way.

Right down the street from Montgomery County is our nation's capital. It was there that a government employee lost his job for using the word "niggardly" correctly in a sentence. A couple of fellow employees—who happened to be both black and blessed with a limited vocabulary— did not recognize the word. Worse, they assumed the guy said something all-too-familiar. They complained, and the literate worker was summarily fired.

What makes this incident so perfectly southern and, therefore, perfectly American is that an investigation by rational people quickly got to the truth. The man had said nothing wrong. The word "niggardly" is a perfectly good word, the offended employees were told. It comes from the Scandinavian word *nygg* and predates the African slave trade. And guess what: The guy *still* lost his job.

To D.C. Mayor Anthony Williams's credit, the victi—er, "fired person" in this case was offered a different city job, but some black Washingtonians complained regardless. "I still find the word offensive, I don't care what it means," one D.C. resident said. Keith Watters, former president of the mostly black National Bar Association, raised the possibility of a conspiracy. He was quoted in the *New York Times* asking, "Do we really know where the Norwegians got the word?"

Now flash-forward to a story in the *Sacramento Bee* in

2001. Robert Pacuinas appeared before the city council to oppose red-light cameras being used to ticket drivers. He believed, as many other citizens did, that these cameras were just another way for the city government to make money. "It is time to call a spade a spade," Mr. Pacuinas insisted, "and acknowledge that the city wants these cameras because they increase revenue, not safety." When his three-minute comment period ended, he received this reply from City Councilwoman Lauren Hammond:

"You . . . made an ethnically and racially derogatory remark and I hope you think about what you said. . . . It is not appreciated. It is no longer a part of modern English. The phrase just isn't used in good company anymore."

The remark at issue was "calling a spade a spade." Councilwoman Hammond, who is black, went on to tell reporters, "It's an old racist analogy and I'm sick of hearing it. This is 2001."

Ms. Hammond claimed to be the victim of racism, which is hardly news. But Mr. Pacuinas, hardly a member of the White Anglo-Saxons Club himself, was simply unwilling to be labeled as such. He went to reporters, who then went to Ms. Hammond, with irrefutable evidence that the phrase "calling a spade a spade" was nearly five hundred years old and had everything to do with gardening and nothing to do with race. Mr. Pacuinas had not been speaking about race, he said nothing about race, he had implied nothing about race, and everyone present agreed that the only color he referred to in any way was the red in the red-light cameras. The accusation of racism was totally and utterly false.

To which Ms. Hammond's reply was, essentially, "So what?" She argued that since she felt like she was a victim of racism, she was entitled to be viewed as a victim, regardless of the facts. For good measure, she added that she still considers "niggardly" to be derogatory. "Any word that has that base word refers to black people, the darkest people on earth."

Once you untether victimhood from the realm of reality, who knows where it will float next? Will Mexican Americans boycott the makers of Spic and Span? Will gamblers be tossed out of politically correct casinos for welshing on a bet? If Councilwoman Hammond ever called the Maryland Smoke Nazis "morons," would that be a case of the pot calling the kettle black? And if it is, am I allowed to say so?

For the existence of these and other questions, you can thank the American South. We invented the idea that offended people have no duty to be rational. If white-supremacist Southerners can be victimized by black citizens claiming nothing more than their right to vote, then any group anywhere is entitled to ruin the fun for the rest of us.

There's no end to the examples of the spread of southern-style victimhood, but one more must be told: the day they banned Santa Claus.

In October 2001, the town council of Kensington, Maryland, voted to ban Santa from his official duties as tree lighter at the annual Christmas tree lighting ceremony. The vote came after two citizens, both Jewish, asked that a menorah be included in the official part of the celebration.

Now, this is a problem in modern America because the U.S. Supreme Court in its infinite wisdom had decided that all overtly religious symbols are banned from civic ceremonies. Therefore, a menorah could not be included. The Jewish citizens countered by saying, "But you're allowing Santa . . ." And so the town council voted unanimously to give St. Nick the boot.

Yes, Santa Claus is, in the opinion of Kensington, as clearly a religious icon as the menorah—a theological position that should offend every faithful Jew this side of Tel Aviv. Santa Claus isn't a religious icon anywhere in America outside of Madison Avenue. He's more a product of Coca-Cola than Christianity.

When word got out about their foolishness, the town council was barraged by complaints. One flustered councilman, asked to explain why Santa was too religious a symbol to be allowed but a *Christmas* tree was okay, insisted, "Oh, no, this is not a Christmas tree. This is an entirely *secular* tree." A secular tree we just happen to be lighting in December. That's covered with ornaments. At an event sponsored by major retailers. With lots of singing. You know, one of those "secular" trees. (Ah, yes, who can forget those winter evenings with your family gathered around a Fraser fir singing, "O secular tree, O secular tree, how nonsectarian are thy branches . . .")

The mild-mannered dolts of Kensington wanted to be nice and take these offended citizens seriously, despite the fact that the nature of the offense was idiotic. Unencumbered as I am by any innate goodness, my reaction would have been very different: I would have tossed these thin-skinned idiots out on their *toches*, shouting "Merry Christmas" as they bounced down the front stairs of town hall.

The result would have been a minor assault violation for which I would have been fined; and a hate crime violation for which I would have been shot.

6

Nothing Gets This Bad
Except on Purpose:
Redneck Education

One result of my genetic rejection of Southernism is an innate bias against conspiracy theories. UFOs in Roswell, secret governments in Washington, virgins in sororities—all such improbable claims I tend to dismiss without a hearing.

I grew up attending church with people who earnestly believed that ghosts and demons were conspiring to bring them harm. They were convinced that their ill health and fiscal difficulties were the result of unseen forces of darkness, as opposed to the half-eaten bag of Oreos dropping crumbs over the unfinished job application on their coffee table.

Today, many of those same church folk live in fear that *Harry Potter* books will lead their children into the clutches of Satan. I am impolitic enough to recall the days when those same worried parents were teenagers who ended up in the clutches of hormonal supplicants at summer Bible camp.

Who has time to worry about shadowy forces of the Illuminati or the Tri-Lateral Commission? My earthbound neighbors are more than capable of putting my liberty in jeopardy during the biannual election process. It's not what the Council on Foreign Relations is doing in private that's the problem; it's what the Democratic National Committee is doing in public.

So, unlike many of my fellow Southerners, I'm grateful for the fluoride in my drinking water, not fearful of it. When contrails crisscross the afternoon sky, I don't bother to wrap my head in aluminum foil. And if I ever run into Elvis working at the Burger King at Lake Junaluska, North Carolina, I'll ask him what Jimmy Hoffa's up to these days.

There is one area of American life, however, that is so irrational, so counterintuitive, and so openly corrupt that I am sometimes tempted to suspect the Bildeburgers are involved: public education

America's government-run school system represents a screwup of such magnitude I am hard-pressed to believe it is a mere accident. Nothing gets that bad except on purpose. My theory: Rednecks have taken over the American public school system.

Let's pause for a quick vocabulary lesson: What is a "public" school? What does that mean? Better yet, let's turn it around: Can you name a "private" school? Harvard? Yale? The Newport School for Obnoxious, Rich Children Whose Fathers Own Yachts? Are these schools "private"?

No, they're not. They are public schools, if we use the word "public" in its most common meaning: a place that is open to the general public. And whether they're parochial, for-profit, or elitist, all so-called private schools are open to any qualified student who can write a check.

We don't call restaurants "private" just because they're for-profit businesses that you have to pay to use. Hotels, bars, stores, doctors' offices, bordellos—all of these are private businesses where one must pay for the services therein, but none of them are considered private. They're public places. In very important, legal terms, they are "places of public accommodation," which means the person who owns them can't even run them as he chooses.

On the other hand, "public" does not necessarily mean publicly funded. The entire state university system is publicly funded, but not just any member of the public may attend. To attend a state college or tech school, you must meet rigorous academic standards—okay, not rigorous, but you do need a high school diploma and, in most cases, an SAT that reaches into the low four digits.

My point here is that we could easily have a publicly funded but privately run school system for K–12 education, and they would be "public" schools. Only we wouldn't call them public because in the twisted parlance of twenty-first century America, a school isn't public unless it's run by the government.

"But, Michael, private schools don't take all the people who apply. That's what makes them private."

Wrong again. I've been to many restaurants that could not accommodate me because they were already filled with customers. Other eateries demanded I wear a shirt and shoes. In my younger, alcohol-tinged days, I was tossed out of an establishment by customers who did not appreciate my 2:00 A.M. renditions of Verdi's "La Donna è Mobile."

When the typical American says "public," what he re-ally means is "run by the government." Like "public" radio (as opposed to those mean ol' *private* radio stations that we're not allowed to listen to) and "public" parks (you know, the ones that charge admission but *don't* have any cool rides?), the issue isn't who gets to attend but who runs the show. For the sake of time, however, we'll use the erroneous term "public schools" as a synonym for "government-run schools." And it is government control of our public schools that makes them what they are today: expensive, inefficient, and incompetent.

In a word: Southern.

Conspiracy theorists, try this: Imagine if the Freedom Riders and civil rights activists of the 1960s had discovered a public school system where 80 percent of the black children never graduated. One where those students who did graduate had SAT and other standardized test scores in the bottom twentieth percentile of the nation? What would the activists' response have been after learning that millions of new dollars were supposedly being poured into those schools, even as the number of students kept dropping? That the number of nepotism-inspired employees kept rising, while the children themselves continued to fail? How would those seekers of justice, traveling across the Jim Crow South, have reacted to this outrage?

Unfortunately, the school I'm describing wasn't on the route of the Freedom March and it wasn't under the jurisdiction of Governor George Wallace. No, you can find this school system today in Cleveland. And I don't mean Cleveland, Mississippi.

In 1998, the very northern Cleveland schools had the worst graduation rate in America for black students. An underwhelming 29 percent of black freshmen had graduated by the end of their senior year, according to the Manhattan Institute. Do you detect racial bias? Don't worry—the graduation rate for students of all races was a mere 28 percent. So when it comes to black kids, Cleveland is actually overachieving!

Where is the second worst major school system in America? Milwaukee, which you will note is also slightly north of the Mason-Dixon line. Cleveland and Milwaukee, two very northern cities in fairly liberal states, and they, along with Philadelphia and Washington, D.C., have some of the worst-performing schools in America.

Not that Georgia and Alabama are reaching new heights of academic excellence, but remember: They're in the South. Their schools are supposed to suck. As a victim of a hideous southern public school system, I fled North . . . only to find that the rest of America was also worshipping at the great altar of illiteracy.

When I first began working on this book and noticing these bright lines of demarcation between the cultures of North and South, education leaped out at me as the most obvious. Down South, the North has long been synonymous with the word "smart," though it was frequently followed by the word "ass."

Northern attitudes about college are so different from ours. We hear, for example, that Harvard, Yale, Columbia, and Brown are popular and well-regarded institutions of higher learning, despite having never appeared in a BCS bowl game. It's a difficult concept for Southerners to fathom.

Most southern states don't have a single top-tier college within their borders. In fact, the southern "Ivy League" consists of Duke, Vanderbilt, and, if you grade on a curve, Georgia Tech. However, we do lead the nation in educational institutions dedicated to over-the-road trucking.

So it's no surprise that our public schools are lousy. All the rest of our schools are, too. But what's going on up North? I thought you guys were the smart ones.

If your doctor had a failure rate of 71 percent, he would be desmocked. If a restaurant successfully delivered only a quarter of the meals ordered, it would be abandoned. If a police force successfully closed 29 percent of its major crime cases, it would be the Washington, D.C., Metro police department.

But every single day, moms and dads in Cleveland, Milwaukee, and Philly are required *by the government* to send unsuspecting children to institutions where we know, we absolutely know, that a solid majority of them will fail. To paraphrase a question I've heard most of my life: Hey, Yankee! If you're so smart, how come your schools suck?

What's more confusing is that you Northerners don't seem to care that your public schools are as bad as ours. If you aren't worried about the kids, don't you at least resent the waste of tax dollars? What happened to northern efficiency? Forget about the poorly educated, overly self-esteemed children (you might as well; the school system sure has); doesn't it bother you that the public schools are such a lousy *business* proposition?

In Newark, New Jersey, the average public school education costs the taxpayers around $14,000 per child. Yet Newark is near the bottom in student achievement. They're paying for filet mignon and getting last Friday's meat loaf—and nobody's complaining?

The one thing I thought I knew about Northerners is that they won't put up with lousy service. Except for the weather, Yankees don't put up with things that suck. And I know this for a fact, because I used to wait tables for a living. Ask any waiter, and they'll tell you that Yankees are the last people to say thank you and the first people to send everything back. They're the first to ask for the manager, the first to complain to the other tables around them, and, to their credit, much more likely to leave a decent tip if they get good service. But putting up with bad service is not the northern Way.

I've sat in a restaurant in New York and watched a customer take out a meat thermometer to check her dinner. I've seen angry vegans threaten to throw food on the ground in Greenwich Village because it sat on the same platter as a piece of chicken. I've seen customers stand at the table and wave empty glasses at inattentive waiters and, once, two guys from Jersey hit an assistant manager in the back of the head with a hard roll to get him to turn around. (I found out later that they knew the guy, but the manager beat the crap out of them, anyway.)

If the cable TV goes out on Sunday afternoon, Yankees don't show patience and understanding. They get on the phone and start screaming. "Ice storm, schmice storm! The Jets are playin' the Giants and I'm missin' the goddam fourt' qwatta!" When city services get screwed up, local pols know northern voters are not easily placated. Chicago politics can hinge entirely on how quickly an alderman gets a ward heeler his trash pickup.

In short, making a Yankee happy is harder than satisfying an aging harem. And not nearly as much fun. Northerners are living, breathing quality control experts who, when it comes to getting what they want, always go down fighting.

But I'm supposed to believe that the same people who speed-dial their lawyer over an underdone steak are cheerfully willing to accept the highly expensive but wildly unproductive public school system for their own children?

Ah, but that's the catch, isn't it? They won't accept it for their children. Just *yours.*

Northern liberals are tireless defenders of the government-run school system, ardent supporters of higher taxes for public education, and shameless hypocrites when it comes to educating their own children in private schools. They are absolutely confident that an open-enrollment, racially mixed, county-run public school is absolutely perfect for absolutely all of America's children. And they'll be glad to drop your kids off on their way to taking Junior to prep school.

Liberals who can't afford private schools move their families to cultural cul-de-sacs in lily-white suburbs. The children and grandchildren of white Freedom Riders who fought to integrate southern schools now send their children to private (mostly white) academies or live in monochromatic, educational enclaves like Rye, New York, and Deer Park, Michigan.

White flight, elitist self-segregation—that's about as southern as you can get and keep all your teeth. Which explains how schools in the North can survive while providing crummy service to demanding northern consumers. These Northerners simply don't see the public school system as theirs. As long as the one school in their one suburb works, the school system as a whole simply doesn't exist to them.

Which is why nobody noticed, for example, when Bill Clinton tapped former South Carolina governor Dick Riley to head the federal Department of Education. Do you know what South Carolina was ranked in average SAT scores on the day President Clinton made his pick? Dead last! Bill Clinton literally could not find a politician leading a more poorly educated populace to oversee our nation's school system. And nobody so much as cracked a smile.

Imagine if President Clinton had chosen the governor of Iowa to oversee the U.S. Coast Guard, or the senior senator from Utah to chair the federal Department of Porn. Such a choice would have inspired a loud clearing of throats.

But our public school system is such an overwhelming disaster that choosing the secretary of education from the worst-performing state doesn't seem all that different from choosing one from the best. Or my choice, not having a secretary of education at all.

"But, Michael, we've got to have a federal education department; otherwise our public school systems would get even worse!"

Really? How? How could the public school system get any worse?

Seriously, think about it. What could be worse than what we have right now? Thousands of parents send their kids to school afraid for their physical safety. Hundreds of thousands of students go to schools where we should fear for their intellectual safety. And millions of taxpayers watch their money disappear each year into the sinkhole of a $400-billion public school system with no hope of either improvement or accountability.

At least the schools are safe, for the most part. The odds of any particular kid getting shot while at school are relatively small. Unfortunately, so are the odds of him getting smart. If you want your children bulletproofed, you can buy them a Kevlar jumpsuit for two grand and save the taxpayers a lot of money.

Not getting our children shot is a good thing. But we're spending a national average of $7,000 per pupil each year, and there are those of us who believe this ought to buy something resembling an education. The least we ask is for the public schools to do no harm. Alas, we are asking too much.

In 1995, America's fourth graders ranked twelfth in the world in math skills, according to the Third International Mathematics and Science Study (TIMSS), and third in science. After four additional years of taxpayer-funded education, those same students ranked eighteenth and nineteenth, respectively. By the time they're seniors, kids in the third-world country of Cyprus know math as well as ours do.

So, my public school pals, if you're trying to create another generation of citizens too dumb to figure out how high their property taxes are, congratulations! You're on a roll!

If the public schools were content not to teach my son math, that would be bad enough. But teaching him to feel great about not knowing math, that's going a little too far. According to a November 2001 report in *Personality and Social Psychology Review,* self-esteem among America's youth has been on the rise for thirty years . . . along with their weight, their drug use, their illiteracy, their pregnancy rates, and their level of sexually transmitted diseases.

But not their test scores.

Self-esteem based on nothing can set people up for disappointment, noted Dr. Jean Twenge of San Diego State University, who made this archetypally northern statement to Reuters: "It is more important that a child actually accomplishes something than that he or she have high self-esteem. Once a child accomplishes something, self-esteem will follow naturally. Children should be praised, but only when the praise has a basis in fact." Dr. Twenge went on to blame this disconnect between performance and self-esteem on classroom techniques that teach children slogans and affirmations such as "I am lovable and capable." "They may also feel that the world owes them something," Dr. Twenge said, and, as long as that "something" isn't a real education, we should be okay.

America: We're ignorant, we're uninformed . . . and we feel great about it! Sounds pretty southern to me.

But wait—fair is fair. When you spend $400 billion a year on schools, teachers, administrators, condoms, Mary Kate and Ashley videos, etc., you're going to get something for all that money. I don't want to give the impression that our public schools don't transmit anything to our children other than self-esteem. America's public schools do an extremely effective job of inculcating some basic principles into our children.

Like racism. Since Slobodan Milosovic went out of business, no institution has done a better job of promoting racial division and ethnic conflict than the American public school system. For example, if you haven't been to a government-run school lately, you probably didn't know there was such a thing as Chinese math. No, really! Remember "Balancing my checkbook is as hard as Chinese math"?

Well, it really exists and is taught at American public schools, along with Mexican math, African math, Italian math, and Polish math, the latter consisting entirely of word problems ending with the phrase "to change a lightbulb?"

This educational approach is called ethnomathematics, which is part of the incredibly confusing new-new math movement (a.k.a. "whole math") that public schools have adopted just to make sure no children accidentally learn something by glancing casually through their own textbooks. According to essayist John Leo, ethnomathematics teaches that "Western math . . . isn't universal but an expression of white male culture imposed on nonwhites." One essay by an ethnomathematician written for public school teachers refers to the "so-called Pythagorean Theorem," as though the relationship between angles on a right triangle changes with the ethnicity of the observer.

According to teacher's guides made available with ethnomathematic texts, math class should accomplish goals like "prejudice reduction; equitable pedagogy; and ensuring cultural equality and empowerment for students." No mention of actually doing math, but who's got time when you're studying how aboriginal tribesmen measure the floors of their grass huts?

Ethnomathematics is on an embarrassing par with "Ebonics," except that Ebonics is a punch line and ethnomath is public school policy. And doesn't anybody care that black test scores on the SAT are lower for math than they are for language? Black activists have long claimed that the SATs are culturally biased. Thoughtful Americans have replied, "Maybe the verbal part, but how the heck can a binomial equation be racially insensitive?"

Well, now we know . . .

It turns out there is a national movement of ethno-modified education for our public school kids. Science, social studies, foreign languages—all are learned differently by students based on their skin color. Some black activists are urging public school systems to open black-only academies so that black children can be taught to multiply and divide from a black perspective. In Oklahoma City, the Millwood public school system goes so far as to teach its children a Black Pledge of Allegiance:

> We pledge allegiance of the red, black and green
> Our flag, the symbol of our eternal struggle,
> And to the land we must obtain.
> One nation of Black people,
> With one God for us all,
> Totally united in the struggle for Black Love,
> Black Freedom, and Black determination.

So let's see if I've got this straight: We run a public school system where the districts are drawn based on race. We use education theory based on the idea that black and white children are inherently different and cannot be taught the same way. Black children need to be taught in separate (but equal?) schools from white children where they can learn the principles of racial loyalty. And all this is happening in public schools *outside* the South?

Somebody owes Governor Wallace an apology.

These obvious, indisputable criticisms of the current education system are dismissed as propaganda by opponents of what is commonly called "school choice," but is more accurately titled "a free-market school system." I am a tireless and unashamed advocate of such a system, due in part to the suffering I endured at the hands of the public schools.

I went to a school that, by any measure, was terrible. Too small for a football team, a choir, an orchestra, or even a school newspaper, Pelion High School (which was also Pelion Middle and Pelion Elementary) offered the bare minimum of classes one could take and still get a diploma from the academic acme that is the South Carolina Department of Education. We had but one high school science teacher, who had to switch physics with chemistry every other year to accommodate graduation requirements. Fortunately she was utterly incompetent in both, so nobody's education suffered unfairly. Our one foreign language offering was French, though the language skills of many of my classmates suggested that English might be considered an alternative.

Our French teacher was an earnest young woman who was very sincere about *la langue française,* but, "C'est dommage!", she also had to teach social studies and junior high biology. As a result, my entire French vocabulary consists of adolescent entendres revolving around the phrase "J'ai un grand stylo."

When I went to college, I majored in music, played in the college jazz band, and sang in the opera program. But as a public school student, I played in a band so small that my trombone and I were often half of the entire low brass section, teamed up with a trumpet player pressed into service on a baritone.

It was a public school so bad that teachers and administrators openly acknowledged its badness. How could you deny it when fewer than 10 percent of graduates were going to college and only half of your eighth graders were going on to graduate? There were no advanced placement courses, no college-level credit courses, and the only targeted education courses of any kind involved lathes and teachers with missing fingers.

The year I was graduated from Pelion High, our school had one of the lowest average SAT scores in the state of South Carolina, which, in turn, had the very lowest SAT scores in the nation. It could be rationally argued, therefore, that I went to perhaps the worst public school in America. And I went there for only one reason. Because I had to.

The government of the state of South Carolina—like the governments of Cleveland, Newark, and virtually every public school system today—forces children to go to the local school to which they are assigned. And here's the exquisitely stupid part, the part that convinced me that the public school system is essentially a southern institution: Just a few miles away from my house, in the opposite direction of Pelion, was Lexington High School. It was a big, new public school with a football team and a real track team and an orchestra and several choirs and literature teachers who didn't need emergency electrolysis. It was everything my high school was not.

We Pelion students heard rumors about kids taking classes at Lexington that gave them partial credit at the University of South Carolina. We saw news stories about plays being performed there, even musicals with musicians from the South Carolina Philharmonic coming out as ringers. Some people even said the cafeteria had a menu—you could actually choose what you had for lunch!

It was almost too much to be believed.

Here I was, trapped at Gomer & Goober High, but my family was paying the same taxes to the same school district with this far superior school. If I could get my dad to drive me over every day, why couldn't I go there? It seemed a reasonable proposition.

That's when I learned what the American public school system was all about. My mother and I went to see my principal, an inept, elderly woman named Mrs. Nichols. A part-time librarian with little experience, Mrs. Nichols earned the principal's position by demonstrating the unique management quality of being married to our former principal Mr. Nichols.

Mrs. Nichols insisted that it would be a bad thing for one of the few kids with test scores at or above the state average to leave this fine institution of learning. She was not willing to sign the paperwork for me to leave, and the only other person who could authorize such a move was the superintendent of the district. She mentioned that she might have his phone number handy, being that they were relatives.

When pressed as to why I would be forbidden from attending a school that was clearly in my best interest, Mrs. Nichols (unintentionally) articulated the fundamental structure upholding our public school system. She told me—and I am paraphrasing here— that if everyone who wanted out of this second-rate educational hellhole were allowed to escape, the school's average daily attendance could drop so low that the school might be forced to close. And did I think that there was some other school where Mrs. Nichols's unique qualification would make her the principal? And where would the underperforming teachers at Pelion High find gainful employment?

Or, as she put it far more succinctly, "Michael, if I let you leave, what about everyone else?"

Yes, what about "everyone else"? Everyone else gets screwed. Everyone else gets an education that would embarrass the average student in Singapore or Sweden. Everyone else gets to become part of the collapsing test scores and widening knowledge gap that are American youth culture.

But the teachers, incompetent and otherwise, remain gainfully employed. Their average salaries are on the rise, faster than inflation. Meanwhile, class sizes continue to shrink. More money for more teachers to teach fewer children, but test scores remain flat.

And, chances are, the children being miseducated by this system are more segregated by race and ethnicity than at any time since 1970. They are being sorted by skin color, taught by skin color, tested by skin color, and if some education intellectuals have their way, will be indoctrinated by skin color. All right here in America the Beautiful.

So tell me again how the *North* won the war? We must have missed that part in my high school history class.

It was taught, of course, by my basketball coach.

7

B.J.U.S.A.

*The trouble down [South], at the bottom, is very simple. That
section of the American people which has the most difficult and
vexatious of all problems on its hands, and not only on its
hands but directly under its nose, is precisely the section the
least accustomed to clear thought, and hence least capable of it.*

—H. L. Mencken on the South and race relations

If Michael Jackson went to Bob Jones, whom would he
be allowed to date?"

This was my question for Jonathan Pait, an able and af-
fable gentleman who at the time had one of the worst jobs
in America: P.R. flak for Bob Jones University. I was inter-
viewing him about BJU's ban on interracial dating, and I
asked him this question to embarrass him. To his credit, it
did.

I also asked it to show how foolish the race obsession
at BJU became when scrutinized. Banning dating based
on skin color was such a ludicrous campus policy I
couldn't imagine how one went about defending it.

So I was taken aback when the articulate Mr. Pait began offering arguments for the defense that sounded eerily familiar. In fact, they sounded like they'd been ripped from the editorial pages of the *New York Times* and the web pages of the NAACP. The more he spoke, the more it became clear that, far from being out of the mainstream of American thought on the issue of race, the quirky backwater campus of BJU was at the forefront.

In fact, everything America believes about race it learned from Bob Jones.

Not that the theoretical mating status of Michael Jackson isn't a difficult question for the folks at BJU. First, there was the ban on interracial dating. Then there was the public confusion over Jackson's sexuality in general. So, even after the administration decided whether or not Michael Jackson is technically represented by the NAACP, they would still have to divine whether Holy Scripture allows God-fearing women to date Diana Ross.

When you're in the talk radio biz as I am, having a local institution like Bob Jones is manna from heaven. Their fourth-rate, irrational theology is a font of embarrassing press coverage. Every few weeks some former student would profess an unnatural lust for his fellow man and show up at a BJU Bible study under the threat of arrest, or some negligent theology student would inadvertently set one of his snakes loose on the general campus population, etc., etc.

On this particular day, the ban on interracial dating was the topic du jour. I wasn't particularly interested in the theology, something to do with the Tower of Babel or the Mark of Cain or the Nut of Job, I forget. Shem, Ham, and Japheth, one of them ignored God's immutable commandments regarding sunscreen or some such and received the dark-skinned mark of Satan, or something to that effect.

What I was interested in was the mechanics of the race-based dating policy. Sure, making a rule that white girls and black guys can't go to the multiplex together is dumb in principle. But try imagining how truly unpleasant it must be for a civilized human being to put it into practice.

First, the university needs some formal, institutionalized method to determine the race of each Bob Jones student. As the Michael Jackson example shows, you can't always tell a person's ethnicity (or gender, for that matter) from a mere casual glance. So somewhere on staff, Bob Jones has to employ ethno-stenographers, carefully tracking the race and ethnicity via some Bible-based formula determining official blackness and whiteness and Hispanicness, etc., along with some method of tracking who was who. Or what. Or whatever. Frankly, just thinking about it gives me a headache.

Then the folks from BJU have to commit themselves to the idea that a student's ethnicity mattered, that two of God's creatures—one black, one white—identical in every way save skin color, should be treated differently and be taught to treat each other differently as well. This requires true, heartfelt commitment from the Jonesians: It's easy enough to engage in such sloppy thinking in conversation, but to behave in such an embarrassingly indefensible way in public takes raw courage. Or stupidity. Among fundamentalists, the two are often indistinguishable.

And finally Bob Jones and Co. must craft an explanation as to how these irrational policies are in line with the dictates of Holy Writ and also in the best interest of all concerned. Setting aside the bumpkin Bible beating, BJU's defense was one of public service: The customers are always right and mostly white.

They argued that the ban on interracial dating was in place at the request of parents who sent their children to the bosom of Bob Jones to suckle on the sweet milk of segregation. Bob Jones's policies were well known; indeed they were trumpeted across the land. If Mom and Dad believed race was all-important, if they had (just for the sake of argument, mind you) an inappropriate concern with ethnicity and tribal purity, well, was it BJU's duty to change their minds?

All of which resulted in this: As a matter of policy, an accredited American university had to pay faculty and staff to break dates between teenagers because they were the wrong color. It's humiliating. It's disgraceful.

Oh, and by the way: It's the official racial policy of the United States of America.

Everything America believes about race, dear Yankee, can be found in the practices and policies of Bob Jones and the old, segregated South. Only now, those same policies and values are woven through the politics and principles of the two major political parties, our federal, state, and local governments, our private businesses, our colleges and universities, thousands of race-based clubs and organizations, and even TV game shows. In fact, one of the few places you will no longer find this overt racial obsession is at BJU.

After the media scorching it endured in the 2000 presidential primary, Bob Jones University unceremoniously dumped its interracial dating ban like a fat prom date. They claimed that the public pressure had nothing to do with it. Then again, they also claim that their frequent references to the Roman Catholic Church as the Whore of Babylon are meant in a nice way.

Don't be misled into thinking this is a defense of Bob Jones. If anyone is defending the BJU ethos, it's probably *you*. You, Kweisi Mfume, Hillary Rodham, Al Gore—the vast majority of my fellow Americans are allied with Bob Jones on behalf of a worldview I totally and utterly reject—namely, the idea that race is determinant. That race matters. That when you know my skin color or national origin, you know something significant about me. It is the one redneck notion that has truly taken hold of the American psyche.

As long as the typical American, North and South, buys into this idea, we're all on the Bob Jones team, sorting the black marbles from the white ones. The only difference between you and the devoted followers of Herr Jones is the color of the marbles you pick first.

Have you already forgotten your census form, your *U.S. government* census form? The one that dedicated three entire pages to questions about your racial and ethnic identity? If any document devised by man could solve Bob Jones's Mating Mystery of the Multihued Michael Jackson, this was the officially sanctioned government document to do it. Start with the six—count 'em, six—categories for race: White, Black or African American, American Indian or Alaska Native, Asian, Native Hawaiian or Other Pacific Islander, and Some Other Race. Then you were given eighteen more "response categories" like Japanese, Samoan, Asian Indian, and Guamanian or Chamoro. Had enough? Ah, but there's more. Your U.S. government then asked if you are "Hispanic or Latino" or not—God forbid we overlook the White/Hispanic/Gua-manian, how would we live with ourselves?

When all the possible categories and subcategories were analyzed, we Americans divided ourselves and each other into 126 separate ethnic or racial clans. In short, it was the kind of government document that only the Con-federacy could love, sent to you by your friendly federal government.

How can any honest citizen deny that the race-conscious ideology of the South has become our national policy? When a society begins sorting the Chamoros from the Samoans, you've gone beyond casual interest. You're like the southern sheriff from Act I of *Show Boat* coming aboard to look for quadroons and octoroons.

So why is the government of the United States—the same U.S. that defeated slavery and promoted civil rights—using Bob Jones University admissions forms as federal questionnaires? The same reason Bob Jones and the Old South did: to treat people differently based on their race.

Oh, sure, the ethno-proctologists who designed the census will tell you it's for research purposes only. They just want to watch trends in health, life span, education, etc. You know, just research.

Then they promptly used the information to pick my next congressman. Yours, too.

The government uses this census data to decide where to spend money on roads and bridges, based in part on the racial makeup of the community. They use it to decide who gets a new park or a new school. They use it to fig-ure out what the skin color or ethnicity should be of the new employee at the local work site.

When a black man showed up to meet a white girl for a date at BJU, the school determined that he was the "wrong color" and sent the assistant dean for idiotic policies to shoo him away.

When a black child shows up at a magnet elementary school that has all the opportunity his family wants for him, but the school is already "too black," the public school administration shoos him away.

When a white family from the suburbs starts looking at fixer-uppers in a downtown neighborhood, the city's "anti-gentrification" representatives shoo them away.

When an Asian student shows up at a state college looking for admission, or for financial aid, the state education system takes a look at her features and shoos her away.

These are just a few of the thousands of examples of formal public policies treating people differently because of their race. And every one of these policies is defended more proudly by mainstream Northerners than Bob Jones ever was by the South.

This isn't just my opinion, by the way. When the 2000 census forms were being planned, mixed-race couples lobbied to have a Mixed Race box on the form so children wouldn't have to choose between the racial identity of their mothers and fathers. This certainly sounds as reasonable as the rest of the census, so who opposed it?

The NAACP, of course. They, along with La Raza and other race-obsessed organizations, fought against an accurate census questionnaire and urged instead an advantageous one—advantageous to their perceived interests of having as many folks as possible check their racial boxes. More checks in the Mixed Race box meant fewer checks in the Black or Hispanic box. These racial interest groups had more political clout, so their less accurate approach prevailed.

If you have any remaining doubt that the purpose of government policy is segregation, I refer to the painfully liberal governor of the excruciatingly liberal state of Maryland, Parris Glendening. When Maryland finished its post-2000 census redistricting of legislative seats, several black lawmakers were outraged that there weren't more black-majority districts to "give black voters an opportunity to participate in the process," as one former NAACP leader put it (you know, because in that racist enclave of Maryland, black candidates aren't allowed to participate without special permission . . .).

Then-governor Glendening defended himself from charges of racial insensitivity by bemoaning the problems created by that most terrible of social trends, integration. The governor wanted the state to create more legislative districts with black, Hispanic, and other racial majorities, but, as his spokesman told the *Washington Post,* "it's difficult . . . where minority populations are not concentrated in any single area."

See the problem? White folks, black folks, Asian folks, all living among each other, shopping together, going to school together. This is a problem, a "difficulty" as the governor put it. What this good liberal wants are more black and Hispanic "areas of concentration."

The Maryland governor's idea is not a new one, of course. Across the pre-civil rights South, there were all-white and all-black communities. "Citizens' councils" were formed to maintain segregation, and homeowners signed restrictive covenants to keep black citizens in the appropriate "areas of concentration." Perhaps Governor Glendening would like to try that idea?

Another liberal Democrat, President Franklin Delano Roosevelt, went even further in creating "areas of concentration" for members of America's Japanese minority. A few barracks, some barbed wire, one or two confiscated pieces of property, and . . . violà! And think of how easy it would have been for those interned Japanese Americans to elect a congressman of Japanese descent.

That's a cheap shot, obvious and unnecessary. Then again, so is the racism of the Maryland state government. (I should add here that the Maryland GOP also supported racially segregated voter districts.) The governor's gripe about the ill effects of integration didn't garner so much as a raised eyebrow from the *Baltimore Sun* or *Washington Post,* by the way, yet another indicator that integration—once the core principle of northern ideology—is all but abandoned.

Let me stop here and disabuse you of the idea that I am preaching the "poor white man" message of reverse discrimination. There are few things as nauseating as watching some redneck high school dropout standing on his front porch in his wife-beater T-shirt, holding a beer, rubbing his belly, and complaining that "them niggers took all the good jobs. You can't get a job if you're a white man."

Right, Virgil. I'm sure the fact that you're forty-two and still living in your mom's trailer has nothing to do with flunking out of the sixth grade, your continued illiteracy, or the half dozen arrests for public drunkenness. No, no, no, I'm with you, buddy. Why, the earning potential for a lazy, gap-toothed clod who can't operate a pencil sharpener without trained supervision must be enormous! It is only through constant thwarting of your superior Anglo-Saxon genetics by a vast conspiracy of "niggers" (probably with the help of their friends the Jews) that you've been prevented from moving up to *assistant* night manager at the Wal-Mart.

If you're a liberal racist gerrymandering congressional districts, you want to argue about racial discrimination and its historic legacy. If you're a conservative racist, you want to argue about reverse discrimination and the plantation mentality of America's black leaders.

Either way, you are a racist. You are clinging to the fundamentally southern worldview that race is determinant, relevant, an inescapable part of the human experience. You divide the world by race, as when you draw voting lines or school districts. You treat people differently by race, through so-called hate-crime laws or racial-profiling police tactics. You view your neighbors, coworkers, and fellow citizens, not as individuals, but as representative members of a larger, ethnic gang.

"All black people should get a reparations check for slavery, regardless of their circumstances, and all white people should pick up the tab." Or: "All black people are bad students in school, disruptive and incompetent; and good white children shouldn't have to go to class with them." There is no different in the philosophy behind either of these statements. They are the ravings of a race-obsessed redneck, and I reject them both.

I reject the premise of reverse discrimination ("The only people you can be prejudiced against are white Christian males!") for the same reason I reject the premise that underlies affirmative action ("Whitey is keeping me down!"). They both start from the same premise as Bob Jones: Race matters.

Which is what makes the constant battering we Southerners take from Northerners on the issue of race so unbearably annoying. I have actually had Northerners who support government-funded, racially segregated, blacks-only public schools accuse me of racism for supporting school choice!

The tendency among the typical (racist) American is to dismiss my rejection of race as Pollyannaish. "Of course, race matters, Michael," I have been told hundreds of times. "You can pretend it doesn't, but it does. Are you saying America isn't racist?"

Of course, I'm not saying that. I'm saying the exact opposite, that the same *New York Times* and CBS television network that helped lead the assault on redneck racism in the 1950s and '60s are enthusiastically practicing an updated version of the same racism today.

I'm not arguing that we live in an America where race doesn't matter, but rather that we have rejected the idea that race *shouldn't* matter. That was the premise of the Civil Rights Movement, that racism was fundamentally wrong. Dr. King summed it all up in one sentence: "I have a dream that my four little children will one day live in a nation where they will not be judged by the color of their skin but by the content of their character."

Martin Luther King, Jr., gave that speech before a crowd of 200,000 people in front of the Lincoln Memorial. Today, every American who agrees with him could fit in a booth at Denny's, where they would wait for hours without ever being served.

The premise of Northernism, as presented by Dr. Martin Luther King, is that knowing someone's race means nothing. He longed for the world where judgment was made on the content of one's character, while Bob Jones and Co. stared stubbornly at the color of one's skin.

I ask you, for the record, who has won this argument in America?

THE SOUTH ROSE AGAIN

Forty years after the Civil Rights Movement, America is committed to the principles of southern-style segregation. Listen to the national conversation on race, and all that's missing forty years later are the dogs and fire hoses.

Glancing through the *Washington Post* in September 2001, for example, readers were asked the question "Is Chocolate City Turning Vanilla?" The piece was written by Natalie Hopkinson, a *Post* staffer who tells of how proud she was to have bought a home in a downtown D.C. neighborhood. Buying this house in a gentrifying neighborhood sent a message (in her own words): "We damn sure are not about to let white folk buy up all the property in D.C."

She went on to decry the fact that white people—*affluent* white people, who are even worse for some reason—were moving into traditionally black neighborhoods. This is a bad thing. "From our perspective," she wrote, "integration is overrated. It's time to reverse an earlier generation's hopeful migration into white communities and attend to some unfinished business in the 'hood. . . . We not only have to invest in the inner city, but we can't let white people beat us to it.

"[My husband and I] wanted to hold a line, stake out our turf," she went on. "As black middle-class parents, for example, we may be more open [than whites] to the idea of sending our children to public schools. . . . Many whites want to help out, too, and their privileged racial status can only improve the city's prospects. But this is the Chocolate City."

The conclusion: "A few months ago, as I left a take-out on Georgia Avenue, a gentleman passed me a flier. It invited me to a community meeting where residents planned to debate the question, 'Is the Chocolate City turning Vanilla?' . . . Not if I have anything to say about it."

Wow.

Now, ask yourself what is worse: that there was a college-educated, professional woman spouting racist homilies straight out of the Jim Crow "concerned citizens' councils" of the 1960s or that the *Washington Post* was comfortable enough with these overtly racist statements that it ran them without edits?

And how could anyone in the year 2001 get away with using the term "Chocolate City"? Why not "Nigger Town," a favorite geographical marker of the racist losers I grew up with? Both are racial road signs reading "Ours" and "Yours."

In fact, Ms. Hopkinson is just one small voice in a national chorus of Americans, white and black, North and South, who long to bring back segregation. In this modern, post-civil rights era of resurgent redneckery, the buzzword of the day is "resegregation," which is a code word for "good racism." Self-declared leaders of America's black community are, according to the *Boston Globe*, "tossing around the word 'resegregation,' using it with a new kind of cachet—segregation without the meanness of the fifties or the fire of the sixties." Translation: There wasn't anything actually wrong with the idea of whites-only and blacks-only public spaces, segregated rest rooms, etc. There was just a failure in the execution. These new black leaders want to have another try at racial segregation, doing it the *right* way.

Who knows, maybe they'll take another crack at slavery while they're at it . . .

The same *Boston Globe* piece quoted Deval Patrick, assistant attorney general for civil rights under President Clinton and a steadfast integrationist, as saying that "integrationists are losing in a fight that was never fair. Since Martin Luther King, we have not had leaders who talk about integration as an inherent value."

And so today, you have segregated dorm rooms at prominent Ivy League universities like Cornell and Dartmouth, not because white students refuse to shower naked with persons of color, but because segregated dorms are demanded by black and Hispanic students. After fifty years of struggle for integration, this renewed segregation is viewed as a positive.

What do the minority students say when you point out they've created the same kind of college campus George Wallace faced off against federal agents to create? "They call it separatism when a bunch of minority students decide to live together," one black senior at the University of Massachusetts told a reporter. "But I have lots of white friends who come here and hang out with us."

Hey, you've got a lot of white friends! That's great. And let me guess: You'd let your sister date a white guy, too. That Rocky Graziano—what a fighter!

Erran Matthews from a segregated dorm at Cornell didn't stoop to the "I have a [fill in ethnic blank] friend" argument, but he echoed another old southern platitude when he said segregation was about wanting "a place to feel at home. Everybody wants to go 'home' sometimes."

If you're a believer in what would have once been considered northern-style integration, it gets worse: The Reverend Raymond Hammond, president of the Ten-Point Coalition, an umbrella organization of Boston ministers, says that while he and his organization don't want a "*legally* mandated separate-but-equal society" (emphasis added), he believes "a community works best economically, educationally, and socially if it stays together."

Ah, yes: another all-black, racially segregated community for integration.

It should be obvious to all concerned that this is warmed-over Jim Crow served from the other side of the plate. Can anyone argue that the rejection of integration and acceptance of segregation (the "good" kind) is a triumph of 1960s northern, liberal values? No, this is Confederate theology swallowed whole and spit up again, twice as ugly.

I say it's uglier because, quite frankly, we ought to know better. My grandmother, who was born in 1912 and lived her whole life sharecropping in rural South Carolina, used the word "nigger" nearly every day, sometimes with malice and sometimes without. But she didn't grow up with the memory of a martyred Martin Luther King, Jr., and she couldn't benefit from forty years of intense public struggle over the ridiculousness of racial obsession.

You and I have. We've had Selma and Greensboro and the Boston bus riots and the Skokie Nazis and a thousand real-life parables to instruct us. If there was one idea of the solid South upon which a family-sized can of whoop-ass had been dumped, if there was one form of southern stupidity that should have been reduced to rubble in the struggle, it was the southern approach to race. And yet it is the one idea that is most clearly triumphant across the land.

The triumph of racism is the supreme accomplishment of the Redneck Nation.

The defense of our new love of racism is inevitably some version of "fighting fire with fire." The timid counterargument from supporters of segregation and racial quotas is that we need Chocolate City or Hispanic Haven or Indigenous People's Island because our entire society is an oppressive, white, European pressure cooker. Black, brown, and citizens of various hues must escape this dominant culture to protect themselves from the debilitating forces always present.

It cannot be said too often that, yes, racism is alive in America. And there is another inescapable truth, which is that it is harder in America today to be black than it is to be white. But adopting the war aims of your enemy means that the bad guys are always going to win, regardless of the outcome. This is why people who want to defeat racism should return to the idealism of the Freedom Riders and become actual "anti-racists." Racism will die when the southern ideas that underpin it are rejected, not before.

Unfortunately, there are Americans who are trying to talk me, Michael Graham, into becoming a racist—and they think every other geeky white boy should, too.

Don't laugh. Okay, go ahead and laugh, but some very

earnest people are very sincere in their belief that white Americans need to learn to love our inner honkies.

Just ask Jeff Hitchcock of the Confederate State of New Jersey. He runs the Center for the Study of White America, where he argues that the road to racial harmony is through more racism. Hitchcock wants his fellow Caucasians to "embrace their own culture while abandoning the privileges that come with it."

C'mon, white people—you know the privileges he's talking about: the reserved parking at Starbucks, the discounts on Wonder bread and mayonnaise, free long distance on all calls to Utah. And all those free short-sleeve button-down shirts. Ah, the good life!

According to the Associated Press, Jeff Hitchcock is "an avowed anti-racist—a diversity consultant who has been married for more than 15 years to a black woman and argues strongly for the United States as a multiracial melting pot." He's part of the burgeoning "white studies" movement in American academia that is currently thriving at places like UC Berkeley, Northwestern, and Harvard.

Charley Flint, a professor of sociology at William Paterson College in Wayne, New Jersey, and Hitchcock's wife, explains the goal of "whiteness studies" succinctly: "We want to *racialize* whites. How can you build a multiracial society if one of the groups is white and *it doesn't identify itself as a race?*" (emphasis added). Instead, Hitchcock told the *Chicago Tribune*, "White people need to develop a sense of pride not based on saying we're superior, but based on the fact that we're working on building a multiracial society."

And this guy is an "anti-racist"? I'd hate to see what you have to do in the papers these days to become a racist.

What he and his fellow faux liberals want me to do is exactly the same thing my fellow Southerners tried to get me to do the entire time I was growing up: become a proud member of the white race.

It is a shame we lack the technology to send the good doctor Hitchcock back to the civil rights era so he could explain to the liberals of the day why the whites agitating for "white identity" in "white citizens' committees" were right. Think of all the time and trouble it would have saved America.

Yes, Hitchcock opposes white supremacy, but the rest of the southern agenda is his—namely, white differentiation, a splintered, racially conscious society of segregated ethnic groups, all very self-aware and ever divided.

I remember once in high school an indignant classmate angered by some comment I made insulting to rednecks asked, "Aren't you proud to be white?" I was taken aback because, quite honestly, it had never occurred to me that I ought to be. Later, as a stand-up comedian, I got into an argument with a black comedian about why every white person should be ashamed of his race. Once again, the thought hadn't crossed my mind.

Just recently, a family member who had her Irish up (literally) over the politics of moving the Confederate flag from the South Carolina capitol groused at me, "I'm proud to be part Irish, aren't you?" In fact, I hadn't known until then that I *was* part Irish. But the answer was again no.

Why would I be proud of my pigment? Where is the joy in the gene pool? Why would I believe I had some significant bond with a stranger merely because we're both pale, vulnerable to skin cancer, and really bad dancers?

Instead of creating a community of color, as the "white

studies" movement hopes to do, why can't we stick with a community of ideas? I am a proud member of that community. It's called America. Anyone who can grasp, agree with, and defend the ideas of liberty, equality, and justice that our nation was founded on (and continues to seek imperfectly many years later) can be an American.

And being an American is, for me, sufficient. At times, it almost seems a luxury.

On the other hand, it's been my experience that people who are the most focused on their group identity are least invested in our shared national interest. Right after the September 11 terrorist attacks on New York and Washington, I got an outrageous, angering e-mail from a die-hard Confederista celebrating the fact that the terrorist attacks had occurred up North and not in his "southern homeland."

At the same time, support for the war against terror was weaker among black Americans than among any other ethnic group—including Arabs. According to a survey by the Pew Research Center for People and the Press, one in three black Americans was either opposed to the war against Al Qaeda or undecided. Among white Americans, fewer than one in five withheld their support.

The Confederate-flag wavers and militant black Americans may despise each other, but they have an important common trait: a divided loyalty to the United States. One states it as "American by birth, southern by the grace of God," and the other reveals it in his self-identity: "African," then "American."

Less than a month after the 9/11 attacks, for example, the president of the Durham, North Carolina, chapter of the NAACP announced that the attacks against America "were not an attack on freedom," since America is not a free country. "Those black males who make it back home alive from war are likely to come home and be discriminated against by the [very] people whose businesses were headquartered in the World Trade Center," Curtis Gatewood said. The national NAACP denounced him for these comments, but the local chapter supported him.

About that same time, the infamous "Florida firefighter flag" flap occurred in which three firefighters announced their opposition to riding on fire trucks draped in American flags honoring the World Trade Center fallen. While the story was wildly misreported at the time, the fundamental facts were that three Americans—black, politically engaged firefighters—voiced their opposition to the flag as a symbol because, according to one of the firefighters, "it represents a nation of oppression," it is not a symbol of justice, and "because America hasn't apologized for slavery."

This was one week—just one week—after the horrific pictures of the World Trade Center collapse and the deaths of more than 340 of their fellow firefighters. Think of the strength of your opposition to the American flag and your ambivalence toward your fellow Americans for you to stand up that week and say, "I won't honor the fallen by flying this flag today."

This is an inevitable consequence of southern-style racism, including the "good" kind.

Spend a Memorial Day weekend in Vicksburg, Mississippi, where the original Confederate Memorial Day is still observed, not the Yankee one, and you'll see it there, too. Recall the words of John C. Calhoun, the great white southern hope himself: "Union—next to our liberty, most dear." That liberty was the freedom of the South to maintain the slave economy and, if necessary, bail out of the Constitution.

Southerners, especially southern whites, are always ready for a scrap, and we honor and admire military service more than most Americans. But there is at our core, and solidly in our southern character, an ambivalence about our national government and identity. We're Southerners, by God, and, oh sure, we're Americans, too. But it is our southern identity that provides our passion.

Northernism was the rejection of the "American by birth, southern by the grace of God" mentality. Northernism sought to drag the South into the American whole, at least in the realm of ideas: a color-blind society seeking one-size-fits-all justice pursued through powerful ideas that are greater than any sectional or ethnic consideration.

Today, no idea is more powerful in the public sphere than that of race. Just as it did in the pre-Civil War South and the Jim Crow era after that, group identity and race obsession have trumped all else. Reason, rationality, not even love of country can overcome them.

And what kind of country is this where race triumphs over all? It is America, the Redneck Nation.

8

Without Merit

Any man can bear injustice. What stings is justice.

—H. L. Mencken

One of the reasons I left the South was to go somewhere I could get fired.

And in the American South, it is nearly impossible to be declared too stupid to keep a job. The typical Southerner might get fired for showing up drunk, for leaving work early, for slipping a hand in the till or under the boss's daughter's sweater. But he won't get fired merely for being intellectually incapable of completing his assigned duties.

Imagine an entire country run by the Department of Motor Vehicles and you get the idea.

I mention the DMV for two reasons: It is a branch of government roundly agreed upon to be the acme of ineptitude; and it is the only branch of democracy I know of that has proven concretely that government workers can't handle shit.

Literally.

The proof can be found on the floor and furnishings of a South Carolina Department of Motor Vehicles office near Spartanburg. The story began in the fall of 2001 when an elderly man showed up at the DMV to get a new driver's license. After he and his daughter stood in line for about an hour, the gentleman proceeded to have a bowel movement in the middle of the DMV.

The man, it turned out, suffered from incontinence. Soon, the hundred or so people waiting in line began suffering, too. There was an unpleasant odor in the air and telltale droppings on the carpet. Apparently this gentleman was too embarrassed to go to the store and buy a bag of Depends, but not too embarrassed to take a dump in a roomful of angry strangers waiting to renew their tags.

Some people gagged. Others left the building in disgust. Something had to be done, and, according to David Burgis, deputy director in charge of South Carolina's DMV offices, immediate action was taken. The DMV official on site asked the daughter to take her father to the rest room and clean things up. But because the DMV would not guarantee their place in line, she refused. So the official, faced with nauseated taxpayers and numerous, obvious health code violations, did what any good state employee would do: He walked back to his office and sheepishly closed the door behind him.

As a result of this brilliant crisis-management strategy, the old man and the feces continued to make their way through the line for another hour, dropping excess nitrogen in their wake. Which meant that every taxpaying citizen who walked into the DMV offices for the rest of the day also had to walk through another person's poop to do their business (pardon the pun) with the state government.

Now, don't get the idea that these state employees did nothing at all as their customers tiptoed through this manure minefield. After the incontinent-yet-legally-permitted-to-drive-heavy-machinery gentleman left, "DMV workers changed the line configuration and taped off a chair where the man had been sitting so other customers could avoid the fecal matter the man spread over several areas of the room," according to the *Spartanburg Herald-Journal*. Other employees helpfully suggested that folks getting their driver's license photos should "watch where you step."

Two and a half hours later when the DMV office closed for the day, the poop was all still there. These government workers never cleaned it up. Ever. It wasn't until the janitorial service showed up that the mess was finally handled.

Two and a half hours of shit. Two and a half hours of paid employees watching citizens stepping around shit. Two and a half hours of a senior manager not doing shit. But would you care to guess how many of the state employees involved were fired?

None. Zero. Zippo. Nada. Not only was there not a summary execution, but commendations were handed out. The boss, Mr. Burgis, went out of his way to tell the media that his workers had done nothing wrong.

"You can't keep someone from getting a driver's license for incontinence," Burgis insisted, missing the obvious point that this old man's incontinence kept any number of nauseated and disgusted customers from getting theirs. And folks—these government workers aren't even unionized.

Now, think for a moment what it must be like for the one competent person (if he exists) at this DMV office. He shows up for work focused, alert, and ready to excel. He wants to perform well and he wants his performance to matter. He would like to think that there are benefits to be earned and punishments to be avoided based on his merits as an employee. Instead, he discovers that it doesn't matter if he throws his customers' car registration into the nearest open septic tank, he'll still have a job.

That's the sinking feeling I've known so many times as a Southerner, and it is the part of the Mason-Dixon mindset I find hardest to bear. As a radio talk show host down South, I would repeatedly point out abject, obvious failures by the people we citizens pay to serve us, but instead of hearing, "You're right, Michael! These folks need to shape up or ship out," most listeners suggest that I'm the problem.

"Why you always got to be negative?" one caller asked. "Every day I hear you complaining about how schools are so bad and the government is so bad, and there's all this racism—if you don't like it, why don't you just leave?" When I asked the caller if he thought I was wrong, if my complaints were invalid, he said that he thought I was pretty much right on. "But you don't have to talk about it." In other words, our schools are run by idiots, our lawmakers are buffoons, we're surrounded by wanna-be Klan members . . . and *I'm* the problem.

I have been forced to conclude that, next to miscegenation and interracial marriage, the most fear-inspiring idea in the South is that people should get what they deserve. Perhaps Southerners have an inferiority complex that causes us to quietly accept lousy treatment at the hands of others. It could be that we think second-rate is all we deserve. Then again, it could be an unspoken contract of Mutually Assured Destruction invoked at every customer service counter: I will pretend not to notice that you can't make change, and you agree to pretend not to notice that it took me twenty minutes to order a cheeseburger.

Whatever the cause, Southerners simply will not accept merit as a cultural value. If Karl Marx had dropped "each according to his ability" and stuck with "each according to his need," the capital of the Confederacy would be Havana, Cuba.

Our *Confederate Communist Manifesto* would be sprinkled with ideological phrases like "Who's your daddy?" and "He's good people" and "You ain't from around here, are you?" The social and political system in the South rewards overachievement in the "who you know" category at the expense of those who've invested long hours in the "what you know" department. The notion that incompetence or lack of initiative should impact negatively on one's life is as foreign a concept in the southern states as free love or public atheism.

I got my first inkling of this anti-merit attitude when I showed up for second grade at Pelion Elementary School. I was reading at the fourth-grade level (thanks to my one year in Los Angeles public schools) and was immediately identified as a problem student. How was this a problem? It turned out that, in order to award passing grades to the larvae of local prominentos, the school system used grading curves so extreme they would make Dolly Parton blush.

It was a useless enterprise. The dropout rate in South Carolina was above 50 percent at the time, and the South still has the lowest public school completion rate in America. And it was annoying to the handful of us who would blow off the *B. J. and the Bear* marathon the night before a test and blow the curve.

I tried to point out to one teacher that giving a passing grade to people who knew less than 50 percent of the material meant that, in her own opinion, half the stuff she was teaching us wasn't worth knowing. This was greeted by shouts of anger from the other students: "Shut up, Yankeeboy! You're still gettin' your A, whadda you care about the rest of us?"

I had violated one of the DMV rules of southern culture: Never acknowledge that someone else sucks. It won't matter how stupid we are as long as we agree to be stupid in the same way.

A-SPERM-ATIVE ACTION

Just in case I thought the rejection of meritocracy was merely the opinion of ignorant schoolkids, there was U.S. Senator Strom Thurmond.

Of course, I'm not going to speak negatively of Strom Thurmond. As a Southerner and a South Carolinian, I am bound by oath and office to love Strom. He's seen so much history being made on the floor of the Senate—the Clinton impeachment, the Civil Rights Act, the stabbing of Julius Caesar—and he's an amazing physical specimen.

Did you know that before he became a senator, Strom Thurmond participated in the Normandy invasion? Yep, he was there, along the Saxon line in 1066 . . .

Seriously, though, it is a little-known fact that Strom Thurmond participated in the Allied invasion of Normandy in 1944. In fact, he was the *oldest* American to take part in the attack. That's right: Sixty years ago he was already the oldest guy in the room.

When Strom Thurmond turned forty-four, he married a twenty-two-year-old Miss South Carolina beauty pageant contestant. When Strom Thurmond turned sixty-six, he married a twenty-two-year-old Miss South Carolina pageant contestant.

When Strom Thurmond turned eighty-eight. . . . nobody wanted to be Miss South Carolina. They had to cancel the entire contest.

It's easy to mock Strom Thurmond for having run for president in 1948 on a platform of keeping the Negro "out of our homes, our schools, our churches, and our places of recreation." It's easy to mock Strom Thurmond for saying thirty years later that "I have done more for black people than any other person in the nation, North or South." It's easy to mock Strom Thurmond for insisting on running for a seventh term at the age of eighty-eight and an eighth term at the age of ninety-four, when his largest campaign contributors were funeral homes and the corporate manufacturers of Depends undergarments.

It's easy to mock Strom Thurmond . . . but down South, nobody does.

Okay, I do. But the reaction of my fellow South Carolinians is violently negative. Everybody votes for Ol' Strom. Just don't ask them why.

A political campaign is supposed to be an argument about what is best for you, the voter. "Elect me," the candidates claim, "and I will make you richer, happier, stronger, faster." For twenty years, it has been impossible to make such an argument for voting for Strom Thurmond, and for twenty years, my fellow South Carolinians did it, anyway.

In his last two elections, it was impossible for the Thurmond camp to argue that their candidate was going to do anything about crime or taxes or teenage pregnancy (well, actually . . .) because it was impossible to argue he was going to do *anything at all*.

They were left with campaign slogans like: "Strom Thurmond: Getting Out Of Bed For Over 98% of a Century!" Or "Strom: He'll PROBABLY Show Up!"

It's the ultimate political strategy: presumed incompetence. And it worked.

Like the drunkard stumbling toward his waiting car or the secretary pulling into the parking space outside her married boss's motel room, the last thing Southerners wanted to discuss was whether or not what they were doing made sense. It didn't matter if Strom was capable of doing the job. They were going to vote for Thurmond even if they had to follow him to the graveyard to do it.

The exclamation point on this telling example of southern-style "meritocracy" in action was when Senator Thurmond's twenty-nine-year-old son, Strom Thurmond, Jr., was appointed South Carolina's U.S. attorney. Lil' Strom, as he is affectionately known, had been out of law school for less than three years when he was nominated for the job. When asked about his experience in prosecuting federal law (he had none), Lil' Strom could only point to the seven cases he had tried as an assistant county prosecutor. His biggest? Felony shoplifting.

International terrorists, beware!

What makes this story quintessentially southern is that not a single political leader of either party objected. The kid was clearly and utterly inexperienced but, thanks to a unique job set-aside program known as A-Thurm-ative Action, his gene pool résumé got him the job while folks with twenty years as assistant A.G.s muttered quietly in their cubicles.

Now, I know all you northern readers are laughing at this ludicrous nonsense, as well you should. This is exactly the kind of inbred, good-ol'-boy nepotism I wanted to get away from. So I left the South and went to Chicago.

Yes, Chicago, where city politicians live by the Daley Creed: If you can't trust your family, whom can you trust?

Chicago, where the cemetery walls are topped with barbed wire each November in a vain attempt to slow down the dead on their way to the polls.

Chicago, where every applicant for city employment is overqualified and underpaid. And if you don't believe them, ask their cousin, the alderman.

But why pick on Chicago? This machine-style, back-slapping politics can be seen in nearly every major northern city. It's how business gets done, how votes get bought and paid for. That's different from the Strom standard. In Chicago, Daleys get reelected because they deliver. Thurmond's repeated elections don't represent a triumph of constituent services, but rather the triumph of "my daddy knows your daddy," the ultimate defeat of "what you know" by the forces of who you know. During the military base closings of the 1990s, South Carolina had the largest per capita job loss of any state in the country—and Thurmond was the chairman of the Senate Armed Services Committee!

WITH A NAME LIKE "KENNEDY" . . .

Perhaps the best example in the nation of "Who's your daddy?" politics is the state of Massachusetts, where to be a successful candidate you must either (a) be intelligent, articulate, honest, and capable or (b) be named "Kennedy."

This rule also applies in Maryland and New York, and it might even have worked in Illinois if William Kennedy Smith hadn't learned constituent services in a South Florida bar from his uncle Ted.

The poster child for flagrant mediocrity being overcome by family name has to be the congressman from Rhode Island, Patrick Kennedy. To begin with, you know you're a second-rate Kennedy when you have to carpetbag in Rhode Island. What, is Delaware too big a challenge?

A profile of Congressman Kennedy in the *Weekly Standard* offers this pithy, insightful comment he made on the issue of eliminating racism in the armed services: "So what happens is, things don't get reported because, you know, let's not make much to do about nothing, so to speak. One of the worries I have about, you, a really zero-defect mentality with respect to defect—I'm not talking now—I mean everyone can acknowledge that if there's a little bit of extremism, I'm not saying that that isn't just grounds for you know, expulsion from the military. But how do we address the broader issues ... Can you answer that in terms of communication?"

Ah, those Irish boys and their gift of the blarney ...

Patrick Kennedy's lightweight status is even the subject of a documentary that has aired on PBS. (Note: When you're a liberal so dim the folks in public broadcasting feel the need to comment, you're an idiot.) Everyone who's seen *Taking On the Kennedys,* the hilarious documentary on Patrick Kennedy's first run for Congress, knows what a vacuous caricature he is. Were his name Patrick Smith or Pat Jones, he would be lucky to get elected programs chairman of the Pawtucket Kiwanis. But as a Kennedy, he's in like Flynn (if I'm allowed to use this expression about a person of Irish descent).

The point here isn't that the people of Rhode Island have a congressman who's not too bright. The point is that northerners in Boston, Providence, Annapolis, and Albany have happily joined the ranks of the "who you know" America I fled in my youth. That trend is particularly felt in New York.

The words "New York" are charged with a magic based on the belief that anything can happen to anybody in a city that exists for everyman. New York is a bastion of accomplishment, a tabula rasa town where nobody cares what your last name is or who your husband is or what your connections are. You're in New York now—you gotta deliver. The City That Never Sleeps calls out across the nation to individuals of achievement and says, "Come show me your best!"

And who to better exemplify that New York spirit of individual accomplishment than U.S. Senator Hillary Rodham Clinton!

[Wait for mocking laughter to subside. Continue.]

Before being elected senator by 55 percent of the New York State electorate, Hillary Clinton had a list of personal achievements so impressive it need not be recounted here, even if I could think of one. Here's a woman who, despite having never held elective office, had a public record so well known she had to run for Senate in a state she'd never lived in, a thousand miles from the people who knew her best. And if there were ever a politician who did not depend on her last name for success, it was U.S. Senate candidate Hillary Rodham What's-Her-Name.

Hillary Clinton wasn't elected in a wave of southern-style, good-ol'-boy, "I-voted-for-her-husband" politicking, of course not! I'm shocked at the suggestion, really. She earned her position of power through merit, experience, and accomplishment. If you don't believe it, apply this simple test:

Imagine her as Hillary Rodham Jones, wife of prosperous Arkansas poultry processor William Jefferson Jones. All things being equal (money, party affiliation, hairstyle), wouldn't Senate candidate Hillary Jones—who had never lived in New York, never held public office, worked at a second-tier law firm in a rural backwater state, lost one law partner to a mysterious suicide and another to the penal system, and whose one foray into politics had been a nationalized health care plan so frightening it cost her party control of the House of Representatives for the first time in forty years—wouldn't she be just as likely to be elected as former First Lady Hillary Clinton?

Of course, she would. You just roll over and go back to sleep, my rednec—er, northern friend.

MERITLESS CHARGES

Back in my angry, young-southern-man days, if I had been asked why I loved America, my short answer would have been that I loved the idea of a place where being the best was good enough. At the time, that wasn't true in places like the Soviet Union, Eastern Europe, and many other points around the globe. Under communism, party loyalty and personal connections mattered far more than ability.

As a Southerner, I felt trapped in the same system. In my mind, however incorrectly, I saw the North as the merit-based alternative to the Bubba-based southern society of low expectations and personal connections. In the most general sense, the civil rights army that marched across the South was fighting for the cause of merit versus favoritism. The Old South customs allowed illiterate whites to cast their ballots while George Washington Carver couldn't get in a voting booth. The civil rights revolution promised a future where citizens would enter the public arena as individuals, not limited or favored based on their group identity but, rather, given a level playing field in which each man or woman could pursue excellence.

Clearly this revolution failed. America is no more a meritocracy today than it is a libertarian utopia or constitutional republic. I won't even mention affirmative action, which is an open, unapologetic rejection of merit in favor of racism—the example is too obvious to merit comment. When an Asian student with a 4.0 GPA is denied a spot at Harvard to make room for a Hispanic student with a 3.5, neither one is getting what both deserve. But this is America, and we don't want them to.

How far are we from the ideal of individual merit? During the Winter Olympics in Salt Lake City, the *San Francisco Chronicle* ran a feature bemoaning the lack of diversity on the American team. The *Chronicle* bemoaned the fact that 95 percent of the American athletes were white, and, the writer implied, that meant something must have gone wrong.

What? Is there a more pure example of individual achievement than Olympic sport? Setting aside the fiasco of figure skating—where it's still the Commies versus the Capitalists giving gold medals to their homeys—you are on the Olympic team if you skated faster, skied farther, or shot straighter than everyone else. Period. There is no room in the process for diversity, and no need for it, either. A black ice skater and a Hispanic curler could no more be kept off the team by their skin color than they could be kept on it for the same reason. There is—or should I say, was—one standard for the Olympics: achievement.

The 2002 Winter Olympics were marred in a small but significant way by the submersion of merit to considerations of race. But the primacy of group membership over individual accomplishment is so pervasive that the Olympic media coverage at times turned laughable. When Vonetta Flowers became the first black person to ever win a gold medal in a Winter Olympics, reporters were flummoxed as to how to describe her. They couldn't go on the air and say "black person," so one commentator resorted to describing Flowers as "the first African American from any country to win gold at the Winter Olympics."

Think of how proud the many African Americans from *other* countries must have felt . . .

A merit-based America would have a flat income tax where everyone pays the same rate. What is a graduated income tax other than a reminder to Bill Gates from the mighty majority of mathematically impaired Americans that we don't care how smart he gets, we can still take away all his stuff?

A merit-based America would have a national college system that was difficult to get into, but one whose diplomas were truly worth having. Instead, we send everyone who can walk and drink beer at the same time into our higher education system. They may not get much from the education, but most invest heavily in the mastery of the "higher" part. After four years of bad grades and bong hits, a majority of Americans who attend college never graduate. The ones who do graduate end up $50K in debt and have a degree that's worth about what my dad's diploma was worth when he graduated from high school in 1959.

College admissions used to be one way of separating the wheat from the chaff. But now that states are throwing money at would-be students to fill up overbuilt campuses, the slogan of higher education has become "All Chaff, All the Time!" Why is it wrong to say to a college applicant, "Sorry, you don't belong here," particularly when he clearly doesn't? Is it because we don't want to make anyone feel bad (a classically southern trait, by the way)? Well, think about how bad they're going to feel flunking out of the Feng Shui of Barney Fife: Mayberry as Oriental Metaphysics.

Except they won't flunk out, will they? Remember those Partonesque grading curves I complained about earlier? Check out this statistic from ground zero of northern liberalism, Harvard University: More than 50 percent of *all* Harvard students have an A or A- average. It's the Lake Woebegone Syndrome: All the kids are above average.

They must be using the same math in Texas. According to the *Wall Street Journal*, some Texas public high schools have ranked 15 percent or more of their students in the top 10 percent of their class. This is because college admissions and scholarships are linked to class rankings, and, well, do *you* want to tell some kid he doesn't get to go to the college of his choice merely because he didn't earn it? That's so . . . *mean*.

The Southerner's rejection of merit may have found its most extreme expression in the northern, liberal enclaves like Oakland and Boston where, along with some seventy other communities, so-called living-wage laws have been implemented. Businesses who wish to bid on government contracts are required to pay all of their employees a government-ordered "living wage," which tends to be in the ten- to fourteen-dollar-an hour range.

The premise of the living-wage movement is that you deserve to be paid enough to support a family of four, whether or not you are capable of earning it. I suppose it would be futile at this point in American history to ask why you have a family of four to begin with if you don't have enough money to feed them. And I assume it would be considered rude to point out that there are millions of Americans who earn at least fourteen dollars an hour and sometimes much, much more, and that their employers happily pay these exorbitant wages without the threat of arrest. These employees get their "living wage" the old-fashioned way: They earn it.

Perhaps it's my poor upbringing, but I cannot see past the vast chasm between what a job is worth and what a worker is paid to do it. It simply isn't worth fourteen dollars an hour to pay a recovering alcoholic to sit in a parking lot and watch the cars for eight hours, no matter what the law says. His effort does not merit that reward.

Supporters of living and minimum wages have the mistaken notion that the reason the boss pays you six dollars an hour is that he's trying to rip you off, that he would pay you less if he were allowed to by law.

This is backward. The minimum-wage law is in place because there are millions of able-bodied adults among us who are incapable of any legal activity that would generate enough wealth to keep them alive. If you are making the minimum wage, it's not because your boss refuses to pay you what you're worth; it's because if he paid you what you deserved, you would starve to death in the building and create a health hazard for your fellow employees.

Think about the term "living wage" for a second: Who is so stupid that they would take and keep a job that doesn't keep them alive? Either somebody who has a severe problem with math or Darwin's next scheduled pickup. If you are too dumb, too lazy, too unskilled, and too unmotivated to feed yourself and you die . . . is this a bad thing?

But America the land of opportunity has become America the place to avoid responsibility. As I write, the newspapers are filled with hand-wringing editorials over the fate of the employees of Enron Corporation. As presented by the media, thousands of naive innocents working diligently for a dishonest company lost everything they had through no fault of their own.

Meanwhile, the story goes, the fat cats of upper management hit the silk and bailed with everything but the towels from the executive washroom. Worse, they fixed the rules so that management could sell their Enron stock while the selling was good, but employees had to hold theirs until it was too late. Employees, good; Enron, bad.

But writer Michael Lewis of the *New York Times* magazine makes this observation:

> . . . there was a brief period, from Oct. 29 through Nov. 12, in which the 401(k) plan was frozen and Enron's employees were unable to sell their shares. The stock during that span fell to $9.24 a share from $13.81, a small step in the long plunge from more than $90 to pennies today. The only shares workers were restricted from selling outside that window were those pumped into the plan by the company as a "match" for part of each employee's contribution. (Those shares couldn't be sold until the worker turned 50.)

He goes on to point out that thousands of Enron employees had to know that the deals they were working on were losing big bucks, and these employees were pulling down a six-figure salary the entire time. Some of the same employees who are suing Enron for fraud manned the fake trading floor Enron set up to impress investors. The investors didn't know it was a scam, but the low-level Enronians pretending to sell shares of Siberian crude certainly did.

These folks were part of a scam, they promoted the scam, they rode the wave of Enron prosperity to its profitable pinnacle and crashed with it at the end. But now that it's over, these same folks—with a decade of Enron-funded big bucks and high living under their belts—want the taxpayers to bail them out. Hardworking blue-collar schmoes who've never earned more than $40K a year should chip in to cover the 401(k) funds of a bunch of Volvo drivers because, according to the plaintiffs, they deserve it.

The Enron employees believe they deserve our tax dollars because they believe that life is a scam. They don't just believe it; they know it—because they were part of a major one themselves. They didn't know where the money to pay their big-time salaries was coming from at Enron, and they don't care where it comes from now. They don't care if the tax dollars poured into their IRAs come from low-wage workers who spent the nineties sweeping floors while they were living large off the Enron economy.

They don't care because this is America. And in America, it's not what you deserve, it's not what you can earn: It's what you can get. Or even better, it's what you can get your daddy, your frat brother, or your favorite uncle— Uncle Sugar—to get for you.

It's just another lesson in economics from the front row of a Redneck Nation.

9

Darwin Is Dead

(And Is Being Channeled Nightly by a TV Psychic from Long Island)

*In those parts of the Republic where Beelzebub is still real—
everywhere in the South save a few walled towns—the
evangelical sects plunge into an abyss of malignant imbecility,
and declare a holy war on every decency that civilized men
cherish.*

—H. L. Mencken

Southerners believe in Satan. Northerners believe in Darwin.

This is the Mason-Dixon line of American religion. It isn't that more Southerners believe in God. Surveys have historically shown that more than 90 percent of *all* Americans believe in "God, a Higher Intelligence or some omnipotent being who resembles Charlton Heston."

What makes America a Redneck Nation is the *way* we believe in God. There is what I used to generalize as the northern approach—temperate, intellectual, and internalized. Northerners attempt to balance faith and reason, Scripture and science. Thus, Darwin is viewed, not as an agent of the devil, but as another truth-seeker whose discoveries must be dealt with directly, head-on. The facts are the facts, and we must trust God that he knows what He's doing.

Then there was the South, where the true measure of devotion to our Lord Jesus Christ was the willingness to be a complete and utter idiot on His behalf. Nothing is less relevant than the facts, and nothing is more suspect than science and reason. We reject Darwin as unbelievable and maintain instead that Adam and Eve frolicked in the altogether just a short six thousand years ago, living in peace and harmony alongside the dinosaur and the woolly mammoth. In northern Kentucky, for example, an evangelical ministry called Answers in Genesis is currently overseeing a $14-million Creation Museum and Family Discovery Center offering proof that God not only created the world in six days but also brought it in under budget through the use of nonunion labor.

Is this absurd? Does this fly in the face of years of carefully gathered scientific evidence? Does it make the parties involved look ridiculous and ignorant? All the better! Simply believing in God isn't enough for us Southerners. Our faith must be off-putting to others and embarrassing to ourselves. Loving God has got to hurt.

Just ask Carolyn Risher. She's the good, southern mayor of the good, southern town of Inglis, Florida. Mayor Risher, duly elected to serve the citizens of Inglis and under the guidance of the Holy Spirit, in January of the year of our Lord 2002, did officially ban Satan from the town proper.

Suburbanites, you're on your own.

Banning the Prince of Darkness from your municipality is no small feat. He is, after all, the fallen archangel Lucifer who once served an omnipotent God and currently does battle with His angels as the Prince of the Powers and Principalities of the Air. Meanwhile, Mayor Risher serves on the town sewer and water committee and has to drive her own vehicle while conducting official business.

But Mayor Risher had a strategy for defeating Beelzebub, one that involved more than merely prohibiting Marilyn Manson concerts. According to wire reports, Risher composed, on town stationery, a five-paragraph communiqué declaring Satan "powerless, no longer ruling over, nor influencing, our citizens." Copies of this missive (notarized, I presume) were placed in hollowed fence posts at the four entrances to the formerly Satan-oppressed municipality, each post painted with the words "Repent, Request and Resist."

That last touch a suggestion by the local tourism board, perhaps?

At last report, observers were mixed as to whether the mayor's proclamation had, in fact, ejected Ol' Slewfoot from Inglis, Florida. Faithful believers commented on the recently improved weather. Cynics noted that not a single used car dealer had closed up shop.

But there can be no doubt about Mayor Risher's faith in the inerrant word of God as found in the original King James Version. She demonstrated her devotion through her willingness to be publicly humiliated. In contemporary America, glaring stupidity is the gold standard of the Christian realm.

Every news cycle finds another band of earnest southern brethren headed to the local library to chuck *Harry Potter* off the shelves or swipe copies of *Catcher in the Rye* from the public school stacks. And if Pat Robertson isn't predicting that monsoons will flood every bathhouse in San Francisco, Jerry Falwell is blaming the recession on the ungodly spending habits of lesbian households.

You can dismiss the book burnings and gay bashing as part of the Christian fringe, but it appears more and more that the tapestry of southern evangelicalism is all fringe and no rug.

Which is why U.S. Attorney General John Ashcroft's "cover-up" of a bare-breasted statue helped confirm the image of the modern evangelical as a clueless bumpkin who would put polyester slacks on Michelangelo's *David*. If you don't recall the story, two statues—the *Spirit of Liberty* and her loinclothed male counterpart, the *Majesty of Justice*—stood in the Great Hall of the Department of Justice. They are art deco works from the 1930s, and for nearly seventy years they adorned the Great Hall as a symbol of our national ideals.

And yes, you could see the lady's booby.

No previous attorney general had ever made an issue of this libertine Liberty and her heaving bosom. But soon after John Ashcroft appeared on the nation's front pages with this bronzed breast giving the AP cameras the one-eyed squint over his shoulder, the Justice Department purchased eight thousand dollars' worth of drapes and covered the offending organ.

Subsequent statements from official sources denied Ashcroft ever knew about the draperies, but according to ABC News, former Ashcroft spokeswoman Mindy Tucker and her female staffers "always hated the statues." Tucker told ABC that "half the women in the department were offended by them and the other half considered them art." No need to lay odds on which half were the conservatives. The order to burka this buxom wench (the statue, not Ms. Tucker) came "from someone in the attorney general's office, who delivered the request to the Justice Management Division and asserted it was the attorney general's desire," ABC News reported.

Ah, yes: desire. The root of much evil, particularly for those easily aroused by feminine beauty. It should be noted that Attorney General Ashcroft is the son of an Assembly of God minister from southern Missouri, and he used to travel the region singing gospel music—a potent mix of religion and show business that gave America both Jimmy Swaggart and Jerry Lee Lewis. It could be that Mr. Ashcroft is simply more distracted by the unclad female form than the usual U.S. senator or commander in chief. He's certainly no Bill Clinton, another self-described southern evangelical who could get more policy work done *underneath* a roomful of stenographers than most CEOs could *with* them.

Whatever the cause, the draperies confirmed in northern minds that southern folks of faith are straw-chewin' rubes who live in fear of MTV and modern art. Ashcroft's action was silly and indefensible. That's what made it so perfect. Anyone can do something smart and sophisticated for God. But to be a buffoon takes a true believer.

Believe it or not, it was my desire to escape this buffoonery that brought me to Oral Roberts University in Tulsa, Oklahoma. I am often asked why I would go to a university whose name is dangerously close to describing a frequent topic on *Jerry Springer,* and I usually reply that it was the school farthest from South Carolina that offered me a free ride. And this is technically true.

But the real reason I chose ORU is that it presented itself as the Ivy league of evangelicalism, a place where reason and deep-seated faith could coexist. Unfortunately the Cornell of the Charismatic Movement turned out to be closer to the Jesus Is Lord School of Straight Chiropractic, combining the intellectual rigor of a Sunday school picnic with the sound theological theories of a slumber party séance. I walked onto the ORU campus a doubting Christian and graduated four years later a confident and confirmed sinner.

Academically speaking, ORU was a disaster. It may have been the only accredited university in America at the time that did not offer a single philosophy course. ("If the Lord had meant for you to think for yourself, he'd a given you a mind of your own, hallelujah!"—Oral Roberts) There was a medical school, but the biology department refused to teach evolution. The university tried to cancel a performance of Gian Carlo Menotti's two-act opera *The Medium* when someone leaked word to the academic dean that the main character was a fortune-teller. Apparently he had been under the impression we were performing an opera about the proper way to prepare a steak.

Oral Roberts's philosophy of learning was the same one I had heard from pulpits my entire youth: Our intellect was our enemy, constantly tempting us away from God's plan for our lives. Increased devotion demanded decreasing intelligence and critical thinking. One of the more popular choruses sung at ORU was "God said it, I believe it, and that settles it for me."

You can see why the campus debate team never made it to the state finals.

But man does not live by buffoonery alone. Another hallmark of southern spirituality is its intensity Southerners have an innate doubt as to the sincerity of northern faithfulness because it comes with so little passion or fire. For the typical congregant in Westchester County, New York, or Lake Forest, Illinois, choosing a church seems to be of less spiritual significance than choosing a country club. I suspect this is because churches have no membership fees, anyone can join, and God allows mulligans. Even in Westchester.

My experience with northern churchgoers is that they believe in God, but not enough to bring it to anyone else's attention. Unlike Southerners, who are looking for the chance to embarrass themselves on behalf of the Almighty, Northerners try to maintain a low metaphysical profile. While living up North, I had the sense that everyone involved in religion was working feverishly not to appear feverish; they were zealously nonzealots. "There is one true and living God," the congregation intoned, "but that doesn't mean we expect you to, like, believe in Him or anything."

The typical Protestant church service north of the Ohio River has all the evangelical fervor of a Rotary Club, except that Rotarians are known to quote the Holy Scriptures occasionally. Having been a music major in college, I can usually find inspiration from sacred music in the most tomblike of settings, but in mainstream northern churches even the hymnals have been neutered and stripped of zest. In one Methodist service, I found myself confronted with the hymn "Easter People Lift Your Voices," formerly known as "Angels from the Realms of Glory." The once-inspiring hymn had been the victim of the "inclusive language" movement led by liberal clerics, and the song featured words like "empowered" and "choices," along with an oblique reference to *Roe v. Wade.*

According to the *Wall Street Journal,* other changes to hymnals and prayer books include still more inclusive names for the Heavenly Being Formerly Known as the Lord. Lords are, of course, males, and usually white males at that, so obviously this would make God a Republican, and clearly, the thinking goes, something must be wrong somewhere.

Thus the language in church services has been changed to attract a larger, Democratic-leaning demographic. The new lyrics refer to God as "Mother and Father God," "Great Spirit," "Daredevil Lover," and, in a tip of the hat to Tammy Faye, "Bakerwoman God."

Northern ministers have gotten into the spirit as well. Instead of sermons filled with fire and brimstone, you're more likely to hear a homily addressing environmental issues. Rather than railing on the swift righteousness of the Lord's coming judgment, sermons more often deal with the need for social justice and Christ's call for campaign finance reform.

It may be one of my failings as a Southerner, but I like my religion served with red meat. When I was growing up, the preacher at my small Pentecostal church in South Carolina would no more deliver a sermon on social justice than he would support legalized abortion or oppose the death penalty. Standing through yet another three-hour Sunday night service at South Congaree Assembly of God, weeping and praying aloud as a frumpy teenager banged her way through "Old Time Religion" on the piano, the atmosphere was charged with purpose: We were shining with the light of Christ, we were defying the devil, we were in the world but were loudly letting the world know that we were absolutely not of it.

We were sincere. We were earnest, perhaps even extreme; Though we never actually handled snakes, we knew where to get them on short notice.

And when the revival preacher came through town, speaking night after night to the same, rugged band of a hundred or so souls, it sometimes seemed I could hear Satan himself scratching on the church house door . . . though it usually turned out to be a pack of local dogs drawn by the yowling. We saw ourselves as warriors in a struggle for the soul of America, and we had a hard time believing that anyone north of Virginia was on our side.

The rejection of reason and the embrace of passion are two of the three fundamentals of southern spirituality. The third is Prohibitionism, which may have begun in Massachusetts with the Puritans, but found its fulfillment in the Bible Belt.

It is no coincidence that Prohibition found its strongest adherents in the South, among the same people who made the only corn likker worth drinking. Modern Americans miss the point of Prohibition. They see it as a cry for help from an incompetent: "Stop me before I drink again!" That's backward. Prohibition was supported by people who thought everyone *else* should stay sober, and had no problem using the coercive force of government to keep them that way.

Southern states have blue laws which, though finally on the wane, kept many businesses closed on Sundays for years and still restrict some commercial transactions. Not long ago, deputies arrested a cashier at a South Carolina retailer for the crime of selling an extension cord on a Sunday morning, thus violating community standards of decency. (Hey, what do *you* use them for?)

Excluding Louisiana, a state settled largely by Catholics and thus considered by all decent Southerners a Papist enclave controlled by the Whore of Babylon, Southerners have always made it difficult for their neighbors to take a drink, play cards, shoot craps, or enjoy carnal knowledge of a lady. Tobacco, being a local cash crop, is different. It is not uncommon to see a small congregation of smokers on the front steps of a country church finishing off a quick butt during the offertory. But in nearly every other area of perceived public vice, Southerners are enthusiastic practitioners of the puritan art of annoying their neighbors.

In the year 2002, for example, a well-respected women's shelter in Charleston, South Carolina, declined to accept any proceeds from a charity performance of the award-winning play *The Vagina Monologues* because, according to published accounts, several board members were "offended by the title." Turning down much-needed money that could aid battered women seemed a ridiculous position for the shelter to take until the local daily ran a listing for the upcoming performance as *The V Monologues*. That's right: just *"V."*

Assuming that the performance advertised was not a collection of great moments from the 1980s NBC miniseries *V* or the twenty-second installment in a series of twenty-six monologues that began with "A," the conclusion must be that a daily newspaper in a major southern city in the year 2002 would not print the word "vagina."

This has got to present quite a challenge for the medical reporter, not to mention the confusion in the movie listings when *D. Tracy* and James Bond's *Octop* hit town.

And so, my northern friend, when you are ready to mock, ridicule, and denigrate the irrational, overzealous, blue-haired believers of the American South, I say, "Mock away!" I lived it, breathed it, and frequently gagged on it. Southern religiosity is a circus of nonsensical superstitions, overbearing zealots, and borderline lunacy, and when it's time to start laughing, I want you to save me a front-row seat.

I just have one request: Don't make me sit next to the tree lady.

I TALK TO THE TREES . . .

The tree lady is Julia "Butterfly" Hill, the St. Joan of the modern American religiosity, who lived in a tree and etched her name in the Book of Saints of our new Redneck Nation. I met Julia Hill on the set of *Politically Incorrect* back when it was on ABC. She was on the show to promote her book, *The Legacy of Luna,* which describes her 738 days sitting atop a California redwood (Luna) to save it from the woodsman's ax.

I was on *Politically Incorrect* to sit in the token conservative's chair, the sacrificial goat for the smug Hollywood types who sit on the panel. If you ever watched the show, you know the format: They bring out a conservative, tie us to a stake, and leave us there bleating while they set the three lefties and Bill Maher (okay, make that *four* lefties) loose to devour us for the pleasure of the twenty-something TV audience.

When Julia ("Butterfly" if you're nasty) and I were on together, the topic was "the environment," which sounds much more profound than saying that five slightly famous adults are going to sit around talking about trees. Which is what we did.

If you could reincarnate the Prohibition-era Anti-Saloon League and the old KKK (back when U.S. Senator Robert Byrd was a proud member), they would be the environmentalists, the pro-choicers, and the Smoke Nazis of today. Trees, tobacco, and the right to choose are the Holy Trinity of the new American zealot. Like good southern-style evangelicals, these true believers are immune to facts and science. It's strange to discover that the typical environmental activist has no more interest in actual scientific research than a Baptist preacher has in the newest edition of the *Origin of Species*.

When the TV cameras rolled, I tried to offer a few facts—the relative stability of global temperature, the reforestation of the American East Coast, the improvements in water quality that have come with new technology. But it was a waste of breath, because Julia Butterfly's position was based entirely on, for lack of a better term, religion. She knows the earth is hurting because she feels it in the Earth Spirit. The trees are being "murdered," the water's fouled, and the Earth Mother is trying to get us to become one with Her and live in peace.

Julia Butterfly knows this because the trees tell her. That's right: According to her book, she talks to the trees. And unlike Clint Eastwood in *Paint Your Wagon,* they did listen to her. They even talked back. Here's how Butterfly described conversing with a giant California redwood in a recent interview:

"When I was [ending the tree sit] I had to leave part of myself behind and it hurt. And so I prayed and asked, 'How am I going to be able to keep the clarity that I've gained up here from this literal perspective that I've had for two years? And how am I going to handle losing the best friend I've ever had in my life?' And *Luna spoke to me for the last time* [emphasis added] and said, 'You know, Julia, anytime you get overwhelmed or feel ungrounded or at a loss, just put your hand to your heart, because that's where your experience is. And that's something no one can take away from you. I'll be with you always.' And that's exactly what I've been doing."

Now, you can call me a judgmental European heterosexual male if you want, but when a seemingly rational human being tells me she has conversations with inanimate objects, I dismiss her as a loon. To me, she's in the same category as the southern Pentecostal who claims God told her to join Amway. So I proceeded to mock Julia on national television under the assumption that the typical American would side with me and not with the young lady who gets career advice from a conifer.

I couldn't have been more wrong. When the show was over, e-mails poured in from people who not only believed Butterfly's story but claimed they, too, had regular conversations with flora and fauna. Who was I to disparage the great spiritual connection that people like Butterfly have with Mother Earth, Gaia, and the Spirit Goddess?

The Green movement in America is one step away from a tent revival. Druidism, animism, shamanism the hard-core acolytes will buy anything . . . except perhaps a can of deodorant. They believe we live on a planet that can feel us, that the woods and waterways are filled with spirits, and that a heaping bowl of organically grown amaranth flakes each morning will connect us to the spirit of the ancient Egyptians.

Looking back on it, I wonder why I was surprised. Gallup polling in the 1990s saw the percentage of Americans who believe in haunted houses rise from 29 to 42; those who believe that the spirits of the dead can return to this world rose from 25 percent to 38 percent; and those who believe in witches grew from 14 percent to 26. Even among self-described Christians, 50 percent believe in ESP, and nearly as many believe in psychic healing. Not to mention the 80 percent of Americans who believe the government is hiding the truth about aliens from us; the 25 percent who believe in channeling; the 32 percent who claim to have seen an angel; and most bizarre, the 44 percent who believe that "good atheists will go to heaven," though it remains unclear what they'll do once they get there.

This isn't religious conviction; it's nuttery of the first order. It's theology as understood by the God-fearing Christians back home who also carried rabbit's feet and claimed to know spells that could cure warts.

That's why I find it hard to share the dismissive attitude Northerners have about Southerner evangelicals and born-again Christians. Do you know how exasperating it is to have a New Ager make fun of your religion? As a graduate of Oral Roberts, I am a magnet for people who want to talk about their spiritual beliefs and/or their loathing of Christianity. My ORU experience was part of my stand-up comedy act, and it was not uncommon to be harangued after the show by audience members who wanted to get their licks in against organized religion.

After a set at a hotel in Washington State, I was dragged into a long, drawn-out discussion with a graying, balding New Ager who just couldn't get over my evangelical background. "You seem so smart," he kept saying. "How could you buy into that stuff?"

Here's a guy wearing a crystal around his neck to open up his chakra, who thinks that the spirit of a warrior from the lost city of Atlantis is channeled through the body of a hairdresser from Palm Springs, and who stuffs magnets in his pants to enhance his aura, and he finds evangelicalism an insult to his intelligence. I ask you: Who's the redneck?

Come to think of it, I'm not sure if this guy—who believed in reincarnation, ghostly hauntings, and the eternal souls of animals—actually believed in God. It's not uncommon for Northerners, especially those who like to use the word "spirituality," to believe in all manner of metaphysical events, while not believing in the Big Guy. "Religious" people go to church and read the Bible, and Northerners view them as intolerant, ill-educated saps. "Spiritual" people go hiking, read Shirley MacLaine or L. Ron Hubbard, and are considered rational, intelligent beings.

What the modern American believer has in common with the fervent Southerners I grew up with is a wholehearted rejection of reason. He feels no need to explain where his beliefs come from, or what evidence he's discovered that led him to these beliefs, or even that these beliefs make any sense. Mock the Pentecostal preacher denouncing eyeliner and lipstick as toys from the devil's rumpus room if you must, but at least he is bound at some point by the text of the Bible. He's not going to publicly advocate theft, lying, wife-coveting, or any other direct violations of the Ten Commandments, no matter how often he may practice them in private.

If he is led far enough astray, he might end up under the desk or under his secretary (or in Jim Bakker's case, both), but he won't be found dead in a new pair of Nikes trying to catch the Hale-Bopp Express. That's for Californians, not charismatics.

What to make then of the New Yorker once married (thankfully, very briefly) to a friend of mine who told me, "I believe in Jesus, and I believe he was God, I just don't believe in the Bible." Isn't this the intellectual equivalent of "I drive a car but I don't believe in the internal combustion engine?" I asked her. What other source of information on Christ's divinity is there?

"I know it doesn't make any sense. I just believe it. I think he's, you know, out there." Yeah, I said, out there . . .

I listened closely for some intelligible belief system or rational thought as she rambled on about her adherence to Buddhism, Catholicism, and (my friend learned later) lesbianism, but she simply wasn't intellectually serious. She wasn't bothered that one set of her beliefs contradicted another. She was unconcerned about claims of exclusive truth from the Bible or anywhere else. She believed that what she believed was true because she believed it. In other words, she was an idiot. But she certainly isn't alone.

The only difference between these folks—Julia Butterfly and the New Age annoyer and my friend's ex—and the gang of God-fearing Christians who put Mr. Scopes on trial in Tennessee is the absence or presence of the Bible. In every other feature, they are the same. Two generations ago, Americans looked down at the small courthouse in Dayton, Tennessee, where William Jennings Bryan and Clarence Darrow battled over the theory of evolution and thought. "When are those Southerners going to join the twentieth century?" Today, their grandchildren in Detroit are calling Miss Cleo for $4.99 a minute.

Actually it's worse. Most people forget that the South won the Monkey Trial, and John Thomas Scopes was convicted of teaching evolution to impressionable Tennessee high schoolers (a dubious case at best given the unlikelihood of teaching the typical Tennessee high schooler anything). Clarence Darrow went back up North to Chicago, Mencken went back to Baltimore, and the Good Lord called Bryan home in his sleep five days after the trial. And what has happened to the struggle between science and Scripture since?

It's been a southern blowout. Eighty years after Dayton, only 10 percent of Americans believe in Darwinian evolution, while 44 percent believe God created the world, including a real Adam and Eve, in a single week, and did so just six thousand years ago. Only one in six college graduates accepts the theory of evolution as true, and, according to Gallup, acceptance of evolution—a virtually undisputed fact in scientific circles—has actually gone *down* since 1990. It's morning in America again for our new Redneck Nation.

I don't mean to imply that a religious nation is necessarily a redneck one. Belief in God is greater in the South than outside Dixie, but not by much. There is a serious tradition of religious scholarship in the northern states, a tradition that gave America Harvard, Georgetown, and Yeshiva.

I'm complaining about the irrationalist tradition in religion that was once predominantly restricted to the South, a tradition that gave us ORU, BJU, and the Alabama Theological Seminary and Institute of Auto Diesel Repair. If the northern tradition had prevailed, America would still be a nation of believers, but that belief would be tempered by reason and science.

Instead, we are now a nation where the number one new syndicated show in the year 2002 is a man who claims he talks to dead people. *Crossing Over with John Edwards* is a televised version of an old sideshow mind-reading act so lame that no self-respecting carny will do it. But millions of Americans tune in to see Edwards, a self-declared psychic from Long Island, New York, bring messages from the Great Beyond to pathetic losers in his television studio.

This is the kind of superstition-based entertainment one would expect from Romanian government television—*Vampires Live Tonight!*—but it's must-see TV right here in our Redneck Nation. John Edwards is so popular, in fact, that he's working on a drama series about a psychic who travels around helping people with their problems. Kind of like *The Fugitive,* except that, being a psychic, he doesn't have to *look* for the mysterious one-armed man—he already knows who it is.

You can dismiss John Edwards and Miss Cleo to the snake handler's corner of contemporary American spiritualism, but what to do with CBS's runaway prime-time hit *Touched by an Angel*? I find the show tremendously significant from a religious perspective; I believe the sudden popularity of Della Reese is a sign of the coming Apocalypse as foretold in the Book of Revelation.

The problem with *Touched by an Angel* (besides the fact that it is hideously maudlin and mediocre even by the standards of CBS) is that many of its estimated 25 million viewers seem to believe it's a documentary. According to polls, about 70 percent of Americans believe in angels, about half believe they have their own guardian angel, and nearly all of those people believe their angel looks like a cast member from *Friends*.

And because of the popularity of *Touched,* the same Americans who snickered at stiff-haired televangelists now happily accept spiritual insight from a former lounge act. Della Reese, or the Reverend Della Reese as she's known in the Understanding Principles of Better Living Church, can't write her books fast enough: *Angels Along the Way, What Is This Thing Called Love,* and *Strength Is the Energy of God!,* a collection of devotionals based on her theological insights as the star of a network TV program. If you don't have a copy, just go to the Touched by an Angel Store website. Once there, you can purchase a copy of her recordings with the Duke Ellington Orchestra, or a CD of *Della Della Cha Cha Cha,* and everyone's favorite, the *Touched by an Angel Sing-A-Long* karaoke album.

Telephone psychics, TV séances, and prime-time lounge singers for Jesus sound like the programming for the Turner South network, but it's all U.S.A. Darwin may be dead and evolution on the verge of eviction, but the Spirit of Dixie is moving across the land.

Can I get an "Amen"?

10

It's a ____ Thing.
You Wouldn't Understand.

nion.

U "E Pluribus Unum" is the defining struggle between North and South. What was the cause President Lincoln found most precious? Union.

What was the reason young men from Minnesota and Massachusetts took up arms against their southern brothers? Union.

Why does it cost $11,000 per head for the New Jersey public school system to crank out ill-informed illiterates? Union . . . Wait! We covered that in Chapter 6.

In 1861, it was the *Union* Army that marched into the First Manassas (and, not to brag, got its ass kicked!) against the Confederacy. The North maintained that one set of fundamental laws on issues like liberty, equality, and the democratic process could govern us all as Americans.

The southern states disagreed. The southern rebellion rose up to rend apart the American Republic, to nullify the Constitution, and to destroy the one nation, indivisible, governed by its laws. They believed regional and ethnic differences between citizens and states were too great to be overcome, even by a document as grand in scope as the U.S. Constitution.

This was particularly the case when it came to slavery, which southern intellectuals of the day (why are you laughing?) described as the "peculiar institution." They didn't use "peculiar" in the "Why is Uncle Derwin wearing Mom's underwear?" sense. Rather, slave owners argued that, while slavery would be out of place in the northern economy and social structure, it was a perfect fit with the unique southern lifestyle. For Northerners, slavery would be bad, but for Southerners, slavery was A-OK, and Yankees, with their more pinched, puritan sensibilities, had no right to judge or condemn the southern way of life.

In other words: It's a southern thing. You wouldn't understand.

Fortunately the North rejected this idea. They argued, with words and weapons, that the Bill of Rights was an excellent one-size-fits-all document and that when the Declaration of Independence says that everyone has certain unalienable rights, it meant everyone, whether they ate southern fried chicken or New England clam chowder.

This was essentially the same debate America held during the civil rights era. Once again, Southerners conceded that their local Jim Crow segregation—with its separate water fountains and whites-only lunch counters—may have seemed odd to outsiders, perhaps even stupid. But they didn't ask Northerners to practice it, to praise it, or even to like it. They merely asked the rest of America to ignore it and leave them alone. "It may not make sense to ya'll," Southerners said, "but it makes sense to us."

America's first multiculturalists weren't Harvard professors or Harlem intellectuals. No, the first fighters in the modern multicultural war were the white Southerners of the 1960s. In the face of northern hegemony, they fought to preserve their unique culture and way of life. As the forces of the great capitalist juggernaut, led by corporate and commercial interests, bore down upon them, white Southerners cried out against the arid, lifeless conformity of cultural domination and urged a respect for unfamiliar social mores in a multicultural spirit of enlightenment and tolerance.

Well, the white Southerners of the 1960s didn't use those exact words. . . . It went more like: "Yankee, go home! Y'all a buncha goddamn nigger lovers! And take them Jewboys with ya!"

The North countered with reason, objectivity, and observable fact. The South wasn't just different, it was *wrong*. It was unfair and unjust for the state or county to treat people differently based on their race. Denying people their rights for the sake of tradition was objectively, observably, and demonstrably bad. So, the North insisted, we are going to use force of arms and federal law to defeat the dictates of your culture and apply one standard to every citizen, whether you like it or not. The standard: reason and justice.

There it is, the fundamental struggle between Northernism and Southernism, reduced to its essence: a single, united nation of melded minds and shared ideals versus a splintered coalition of people who consider themselves unique and unknowable from each other, unable to agree on a single, rational standard for behavior.

Today, 150 years after the Civil War and a generation

after the Civil Rights Movement, I ask you, my northern friend: Who won?

Pal, it wasn't even close.

The melting pot of American culture is dead, kicked over by academics, intellectuals, and individual citizens, all claiming that their heritage or ethnicity makes their way of seeing the world unique. Or perhaps I should say "peculiar."

Hardly a voice is raised in the cause of Union, of a single, encompassing American culture. No, we're all croutons in the great American salad bowl, confederates of a thousand different secessions from the ideal of American unity.

Thus in New Jersey, black state senators killed a bill requiring schoolchildren to recite the Declaration of Independence's "all men are created equal" statement because they found it offensive.

Meanwhile, evangelical Christians appear at local libraries to keep *Harry Potter* from introducing unsuspecting children to the exciting world of Satanism. One of the proud puritans wrote in a letter to the editor, "I'm probably going to be called stupid, but I know what is right for me and my family."

In Maryland, the ultraliberal Montgomery County school board voted to force Poolesville High School to drop its fifty-year-old nickname, the "Indians," despite the fact that more than 80 percent of American Indians surveyed by *Sports Illustrated* do not find such team names offensive. "But if one person is offended, that's too much," said one self-declared Indian leader.

In Denver, Colorado, Columbus Day has been canceled because some American Indians are offended by celebrations of the conquest of North America by Europeans. They instead celebrate "Indigenous Persons" Day.

In New York, some Italian Americans are insulted by the idea that Native Americans are insulted by Columbus Day. Italian American traditions are under assault by Indians who are hostile to their culture, the Italians say.

Meanwhile, Spanish Americans are still trying to figure out why the Italians get all the credit for Columbus when everyone knows that it was Queen Isabella of Spain who put up all the money. Where's Spanish American Day, amigos?

Amigo this, reply American Hispanics. You Spaniards are just European white-boy wanna-bes. We're the real minority around here and we've got Cinco de Mayo, a great holiday celebrating the fact that we kicked Euro-butt in Mexico in 1862 and are probably gonna do it again in the World Cup.

Wait a minute, muchachos, say the Columbian Americans, that World Cup belongs to us. And who decided we have to be called "Hispanic," anyway? What do we have in common with the desert cultures of northern Mexico? We want our own line on the census form.

Damn straight, say the Cuban Americans. Why, Miami was a great town when we ran the place. Now all these El Salvadorans and Guatemalans are killing our property values. We Cubans have nothing to do with those peons, and if one more oppressive, Anglo journalist runs another story calling *us* "Hispanic," we're gonna open up an Elián-sized can of Cuban Whoop-ass on him. Down with Fidel!

And all the while, the hearty laughter of John C. Calhoun fills the cavernous halls of hell.

Less than fifty years after southern blacks and northern

whites marched, fought, and died for One Nation, Indivisible, America has devolved into a "peculiar institution." There is no single standard of behavior, no single standard of reason or justice.

The only right every American enjoys today is the right to be as stupid as he wants to be and still be taken seriously by his neighbors. If that's not a Redneck Nation, I don't know what is.

YOU WEAR YOUR X . . .

> We hold these truths to be self-evident, that all men are created equal, that they are endowed by their Creator with certain unalienable rights, that among these are life, liberty and the pursuit of happiness. That to secure these rights, governments are instituted among men, deriving their just powers from the consent of the governed.

As I mentioned earlier, these words, from the Declaration of Independence, have been declared "exclusionary and insensitive" by the New Jersey Senate. The attack against a bill requiring schoolchildren to recite this part of the Declaration was led by Senator Wayne Bryant, who labeled it "offensive to [the black] community." "You have the nerve to ask my grandchildren to recite these words?" he said on the floor of the Senate. "How dare you?"

How this language is exclusionary today, Senator Bryant never explained. He was never asked to explain. He's learned the key rule of the Redneck Nation: never explain. Just announce that your opponents will never understand.

If the phrase "all men are created equal" is offensive today because it once excluded blacks (and women and non-property owners and people under twenty-one, for that matter), then isn't the term "human being" also exclusionary? After all, there were people who once considered Africans less than human. The prevailing view in America once was that slaves were merely property. Should every mention of the word "property" in the U.S. Constitution be stricken?

We could all pretend that the Declaration was, in fact, a racist document and that these words are racist on their face. In order to take Senator Bryant seriously, we would have to. And a majority of his fellow state senators, much to their discredit, did.

But instead of pretending to believe this sheer, utter nonsense, wouldn't it be easier for a rational person to just stand up and point out that this man is an idiot? That what he's saying is clear and demonstrably untrue?

Ah, but that's the problem. In our modern, multicultural America, it's enough that his opinions are true to him. And really, who are we to judge? Does it matter that these words from the Declaration of Independence aren't actually offensive? Isn't it more important that some people *think* they're offensive?

As any solid citizen of the old, segregated South would have told you, it's completely possible for a word or phrase to be offensive to one group and not to another. So take your damn "Freedom Now!" placards and get back on the bus, Yankee!

For Confederate-style multiculturalists, there is no obligation for any group to explain the reasonableness of its actions or attitudes to any other. Consider again the ongoing fight over Indian mascots for sports teams. That poll of American Indians by *Sports Illustrated* showed that more than 80 percent were not offended by Indian mascots or team names. Surprising to me, more than 60 percent weren't even bothered by the "Redskins" nickname.

This is interesting because you don't have to be a descendant of Geronimo or Sacagawea to find the Washington "Redskins" offensive. Reasonable people articulate and understand why a team name that appears frequently in movie dialogue accompanied by the modifier "them dirty" might be inappropriate for public use.

So when a group of Native American activists stands up and says, "Calling a team 'Redskins,' which has frequently been used as a racial slur, is unacceptable," I can understand their point— a viewpoint I share, by the way. It's rational and comprehensible to anyone. But when folks like Richard Regan of the Maryland Commission for Indian Affairs announce that all Indian mascots—Braves, Seminoles, Warriors, etc.— are offensive, they are uttering nonsense.

Regan, a proud Lumbee Indian from North Carolina, fled his political failures back home to become a leader of Native American causes in the People's Republic of Maryland—a state with virtually no Indians. He has declared community sports leagues like youth soccer and Little League baseball "a hate growth market" because they allow Indian team names. When a school district in Havre de Grace, Maryland, refused to change its team name from the "Warriors," Regan told the *Baltimore Sun*, "I think it's a sad day when the public school system has more in common with the Ku Klux Klan than an advocacy group representing Maryland's American Indians."

Lynching black people, blowing up churches, putting a bow and arrow on your basketball jersey—to multiculturalists like Regan, it's all the same. What's bizarre is that Regan and his allies have never answered the first, fundamental question: What's offensive about a group of kids who want to associate themselves with Indian culture?

Well, my fellow white people, the secret is out. I might as well confess right now. Yes, Richard Regan, you're right: The reason that Boy Scout troops and baseball teams choose mascots is that they're looking for someone to insult. You've been right all along. The reason multimillion-dollar university sports programs choose mascots like Irishmen or Celts or Vikings or Aztecs is to sow hatred and show solidarity with the Klan.

Why, whenever four-time Cy Young Award-winning pitcher Greg Maddux pitches another shutout for the Atlanta Br—uh, you-know-whos, wearing a Native American warrior name on his chest, you can practically hear the cries of humiliation from the Great Tribal Meeting of Indigenous Peoples in the Sky. Oh, the anguish! Oh, the shame! All those talented athletes—white, black, and Hispanic—calling themselves "Indians" or "Warriors" and "Illini," wearing uniforms and logos with traditional symbols of Native American culture as they appear on national TV before millions of cheering fans. I mean, it's not like people look up to athletes in America these days. My God, it's got to be incredibly humiliating.

Which probably explains why the NAACP's favorite college mascot is the Rebel of Ole Miss.

Your heart has to go out to the poor Confederate loyal-

ists, mocked every football Saturday by a stadium filled
with Confederate flags. There, on the field, all those black
players (except the lily-white QB, of course) calling themselves "Rebels," while some guy pretending to be a Confederate officer mocks and demeans the sacrifices of their
southern ancestors. There are even historically inaccurate
and culturally insensitive attempts to sound the infamous
rebel yell. Oh, the shame must be almost too much to bear.

Why, the ongoing insult to Confederate heritage at the
University of Mississippi is so complete, I'm left to assume
the entire enterprise is an outlandishly clever conspiracy
organized and conducted by vengeful black Mississippians
from a secret headquarters deep in the Delta.

And if black Mississippians ever came to a Rebels football game, I'd ask them about it . . .

To think otherwise is to think that schools, clubs, and
organizations choose mascots and team names from cultures and people they want to honor and emulate. To think
otherwise, you must believe that athletes and fans want to
be associated with Braves, Warriors, and Indians because
Braves, Warriors, and Indians represent, in their minds,
virtues they hope to attain, like courage, strength, and cun-
ning.

To think otherwise, you must think that the Richard Re-
gans and Indian-rights activists of the world are total and
utter dopes.

It might, however, explain the fate of the Fightin'
Whiteys, an intramural basketball team started in 2002 by
Solomon Little Owl at the University of Northern Colorado.
Upset by the lukewarm response to his protests over In-
dian sports mascots, Little Owl decided to turn the tables:
He named his team the Fightin' Whites (though the play-

ers called themselves the "Whiteys"), complete with a geeky white-boy mascot. Their slogan: "Everythang's Gonna Be All White!"

"The message is, let's do something that will let people see the other side of what it's like to be a mascot," Little Owl said. "I am really offended by this mascot issue."

Unfortunately the "other side"—that is, the white people of Colorado—refused to be offended. In fact, they seemed to be . . . flattered. "I think it's great!" said one white e-mailer who contacted Little Owl's team. T-shirt sales surged. Rush Limbaugh talked about them on the air. When the date arrived for their first intramural game, more than half the crowd were members of the media.

The Fightin' Whites got trounced, by the way. Apparently Little Owl's multiethnic basketball team even *played* like white guys.

And still the Indian activists complain. The poor kids at Maryland's Poolesville High lost fifty years of tradition when the county school board forced them to bench the "Indians." The students, teachers, and parents voted overwhelmingly to keep the team name, but the elected school board members shot them down. "This is not a democracy," one school board member allegedly told a Poolesville supporter.

Well, not in Montgomery County, Maryland, anyway . . .

Some Poolesville folks asked me at the time what I thought their new mascot should be. I insisted that they follow the dictates of the multiculturalists. Poolesville needed a mascot that was not specific to any ethnic or racial group, and would be popular among high schoolers and promote good values. I made these suggestions:

- The Poolesville Scalpers. Young people should be encouraged to learn about the free market, and the go-getters who snag tickets to popular concerts and sporting events and resell them at a significant profit are the perfect role model. The mascot could be a guy standing outside a stadium, holding up some tickets, and shouting, "Got two! Got two!"
- The Medicine Men. Academic excellence is important, too. Why not honor those students who plan to major in premed when they go to college? Such a mascot would inspire these high schoolers to a higher calling. (For female squads, the obvious choice is "Medicine Women," though the Poolesville "Earth Mothers" or "Juju Women" might also be popular.)
- The Firewater. Sensitivity to stereotypes has encouraged many sports teams to choose abstract concepts and inanimate objects as names. Along with "the Heat," "the Flame," "the Storm," and "the Liberty," "the Firewater" would be completely inoffensive, and it might also spur interest in the team from New Age types.

But the best choice for a new mascot, in my humble opinion, would be the Poolesville High Engines. Young people love cars. They love rockets, jets, anything with an engine that goes fast. Why, just look at the success of the film *The Fast and the Furious*. What could be more inspiring for a sports team than to be known as the "Red Hot Engines" of Poolesville High?

The "Red Engines" for short.

The internal combustion engine has its critics, however, and nothing will ruin a school pep rally faster than a

protest led by Al Gore—with or without the beard. Therefore, I proposed the mascot be a steam engine, say a lo-
comotive. Powerful, fast, and relatively environmentally
friendly, this would be the perfect, nonethnic, nonoffen-
sive sports team name.

Just imagine this scene at the next Poolesville High football game:

The Poolesville High football team, dressed in red,
waits to take the field. From the stands comes the chant
"Engines! Engines! Engines! G-o-o-o-o Engines!" Can you
hear it? Then frenzied fans join in the "Engine Dance," a
cheer in which fans imitate the piston motion of a steam
engine by extending their arms forward and chopping
them up and down, all the while wailing "Whooo! Whoo-
whoo!" Then, as the band sends up puffs of steam (or,
more likely, smoke) to signal the team, the Engines race
onto the field!

From the Indians to the Engines: finally, a high school
mascot that sends a real message. I wonder if the activists
will ever get it?

JOHN C. CALHOUN, MULTICULTURALIST

Advocates of multiculturalism will reject the above examples as fringe, as though I'm overlooking the "good" as-
pects of having a respect for the beliefs of other cultures.
But by co-opting the southern philosophy of "exceptionalism"—what I believe and how I behave need not meet any
rational standards but should just be accepted without
judgment—multiculturalists have gone from merely laughable to possibly dangerous. There is, for example, a theory

about black culture which states that young African American men do not have the ability to understand or obey the law. And because of this cultural heritage, black people should be treated differently in court than white people.

Does this sound familiar? It should. It's a racist sentiment that every white Southerner has heard expressed at one time or another.

I know I was taken aback when I ran across this theory in the *Cincinnati Enquirer*. The defendant in question was a young black man. The person making the argument that he was culturally incapable of discerning right from wrong: his attorney.

The lawyer, Victor Sims, was representing one of three young black defendants found guilty of looting a local department store of $131,000 in easily transportable goods during the April 2001 riots. After hearing his view of race and character, I began to suspect that he was being financed by the Aryan Nations legal fund.

Pleading for a light sentence, Sims first argued that his client was racially entitled to loot whatever he wanted because it was a department store with a large black clientele. As the *Enquirer* reported it: "Sims contended that . . . Deveroes [the looted department store] shouldn't complain too much because the store benefited from those living in that community. 'It's been the black community and these young boys,' Sims said pointing to the defendants, 'that has kept them in business.' "

This is an interesting view of property rights, and no doubt Sims believes that Cincinnati's suburban hausfraus would be completely within their rights to loot SUV's from nearby dealerships during the next period of social unrest. Sims then went on to offer an even more disturbing reason why his client should be spared: "It's not their fault. They wouldn't be running the streets at 2 A.M. if they had opportunities or if government programs weren't killed by budget cuts. We make a different inference for these young black men than we do for better economically situated white males," Sims said.

Setting aside the "Republican budget cuts turned me into a looter" nonsense, the cultural condescension drenching this statement is nauseating. I know lots of people who make "different inferences for young black men" than they do for others. I grew up with these inferers, watched them gather around burning crosses among the scrub oaks of Lexington County, South Carolina, and heard their ignorant claims of white supremacy and the inherent inferiority of black culture. I just never thought I would hear a black lawyer north of Ohio make these inferences, and without an objection from the local black community and civic leadership. But then again, what would the purveyors of southern-style victim status object to? Sims is merely preaching from the gospel of cultural exceptionalism, which is the accepted doctrine in the Redneck Nation.

Fortunately for reason and justice, the judge in this case rejected the "looting as an alternative lifestyle" argument and he gave the looters a race-neutral sentence. The judge argued, as I do, that even if you were a member of a social or ethnic group that accepted and promoted crime and violence as a norm, there is no reason for the rest of us to accommodate your cultural proclivities.

And there are indeed cultures of death and violence jockeying for our attention, as every American learned on September 11, 2001.

I had hoped that one of the unintended bits of collat-

eral damage of 9/11 would be the death of multiculturalism. How could Americans continue to make the southern
argument that no culture was inherently bad or good after
three thousand of our fellow citizens were killed by practicing members in good standing with modern Muslim fundamentalism?

In the days immediately after the terrorist attacks, Confederate-style multiculturalism was clearly on the ropes. TV
ads appeared that would have been unimaginable in the
ethno-maniacal era of Clinton. The most moving ad I saw
featured child after child from various ethnic groups and
religions, each announcing solemnly and with determina-
tion, "I am an American." It was as though our nation's entire supply of hyphens had been wiped out in a single
blast. You could almost feel David Duke and Al Sharpton
cringing in their lairs.

But the loyalty to our Union didn't last. Soon there were
black firefighters in Florida complaining about riding in
trucks flying the American flag, while one of them insisted
"that isn't our flag." (So, can I get you a Confederate one?)
Then some American Muslims began complaining that all
this talk about fighting terror should in no way discourage
Palestinians from killing Jews. And on and on.

If America ever needed an object lesson in the dangers
of irrational multiculturalism and regional exceptionalism,
we got it in the aftermath of September 11 as we tried to
apply Western values to the violent, arcane warrior faith of
Islam.

If ever there was a candidate for thorough and utter cultural rejection, it is Muslim fundamentalism. As practiced in
the vast majority of Middle Eastern nations, Islam is a reli-

gion of peace in the same way that Nazism was a philosophy of racial understanding.

"We understand that you are a Jew. Get in the truck."

Even the most cursory review of the teachings of Islam (a word that means "submission," not "peace," by the way) reveals that, in addition to the encouragement of admirable traits like compassion, self-control, and sobriety, it is a faith that teaches its followers to kill in the name of God. Wake up, say your prayers, skip the bacon, cane your wife, kill an infidel, and call it a day.

No other major Western religion in the twenty-first century allows for the killing of the unconverted. None. The tired arguments that Christians launched the Crusades and have engaged in anti-Semitic violence miss the point entirely. Yes, Christians have killed in the name of Christ, but they have always been hard-pressed to demonstrate that the killings were His idea. Western culture is a violent culture *despite* the teachings of Christ, not because of them.

But look at the nations governing themselves by Islam and its laws, or *shari'a*. These are places where, under direct orders of their faith and its recognized leaders, the government lops off heads, hands, and other limbs in the name of Allah. You'll also find the rejection of democracy, prohibitions on the practice of other religions, public executions for "crimes" like adultery, and governmental support for fatwas ordering the death of infidels and blasphemers.

I laugh whenever I hear a modern American Muslim insist that these nations do not represent mainstream Islam. They remind me of the earnest young woman at Oral Roberts University who tried to convince me that most sorority girls are virgins. They both need to check their math.

Once again, multiculturalists ask me to accept the beheadings, stonings, and dictatorships as inappropriate perhaps for America but part of the cultural life of the Middle East. Okay, fine. But what of the Muslim subculture in America that brings these Neanderthal notions to us?

After the Twin Towers fell, many Americans were upset to learn that hundreds of thousands of Muslims live in America, as residents and citizens, but feel no loyalty to the idea of America. They send their children to schools like the Muslim Community School in Potomac, Maryland, where kids learn that the greatest government is an Islamic government and that democracy should only be tolerated, not celebrated.

In an interview with the *Washington Post,* one Muslim seventh grader asked, "What does it really mean to be an American? Being American is just being born in this country." Another Muslim Community School student added, "If I had to choose sides, I'd stay with being Muslim. Being an American means nothing to me. I'm not even proud of telling my cousins in Pakistan that I'm American."

This school has 150 students, mostly from middle-class and affluent families. Their parents are educated and enjoying the liberty and opportunity of America. And they are paying good money for their children to learn that this isn't their country.

How fascinating it is that these academics have been around for years but until the terrorist attacks of 2001, nobody noticed. Mullahs and imams have been preaching divided loyalties, supporting murderous fatwas, and sending millions of dollars to terrorist organizations abroad like

Hamas and Hezbollah. But until 9/11, this radically anti-Western culture, active right in our communities, never caught our attention.

Five toothless goobers get together in Coeur d'Alene, Idaho, and rant about establishing a white Christian nation and it's a full episode of *20/20,* but hundreds of thousands of Muslims gather each week to discuss the proper context in which to kill the infidels, and it doesn't even make the Metro section of the *New York Times.*

I'm not making the pathetic "The only group you're allowed to hate is the straight, white Christian male" argument. I'm glad to see the media hammer fall every time the pointy, empty head of the KKK pops up. But how did we end up with an America so attuned to divisive ideas that calls for tax cuts are denounced on the floor of Congress as racist "code words" by Congressman Charles Rangel of New York, but a mosque full of Muslims can openly support terrorists who target Israelis and nobody notices?

It's easy, once you buy the southern notion of cultural exceptionalism, which is, of course, the entire underpinning of the modern multicultural movement.

Perhaps it's my inner redneck speaking, by the way, but I have no problem whatsoever denouncing Arab Muslim culture as a whole. I'm not rejecting the idea that there are differences in culture, North and South, or West versus East. I'm rejecting the redneck notion that you can't tell the difference between the good ones and the bad ones, the argument that every culture clash must end with "You wear your X and I'll wear mine."

In fact, I would argue that the violent, suspicious, and ignorant Islamo-facist living in Pakistan or Palestine today is the cultural equivalent of the stereotypical redneck of

American lore. Modern Arabia is nearly a dead-on parallel to the Appalachian mountain society Mencken wrote about during the Scopes trial. They cling almost blindly to their religious leaders, reject the very idea of rational, scientific thought as being necessary, and view every outsider as a threat to the virtue of their daughters.

A year after the Pentagon and World Trade Center attacks—even after the terrorist Osama bin Laden acknowledged his responsibility—media reports indicate that vast numbers of these Muslim morons believe that the attacks were carried out by the Jews, with the help of the CIA.

Gee, I have a handful of callers to my radio shows who think the same thing. They also believe in the Illuminati, the Trilateralist Conspiracy, and that the fluoride in their drinking water is a scheme of the United Nations to make their brains more receptive to low-frequency radio transmissions. Oh, and one more thing: Nobody takes these idiots seriously.

Aha, Michael! You mock Muslim culture for its paranoiacs but acknowledge that America has its own loonies as well. This proves that every culture truly is equal!

Not quite. In America, people this stupid represent the fringe. In the Middle East, the fringe is everyone else.

Imagine, for example, if Pat Robertson appeared on tele-vision tomorrow and said, "I just got a message from Juh-EE-sus, and he said for uh-you tuh go OW-ut and kill all the uh-abortion doctors," every Christian sect would denounce him on the spot. Presbyterians, Roman Catholics, even rural Pentecostals would put down their snakes long enough to say, "Hey. That ain't right."

But educated Muslims around the world openly support jihad terror. Respected imams instruct their followers to kill in the name of Allah. When the leaders of the fifty-seven Islamic nations met in 2002, they couldn't agree that an eighteen-year-old who strapped herself with explosives and detonated them in a shopping mall was a terrorist. Far from denouncing these homicide bombers who targeted civilians, these leaders of the Islamic world promised thousands of dollars in rewards to the families of "martyrs." But as the editor of the *Minneapolis Star-Tribune* put it in April 2002: "One person's suicide bomber is another person's freedom fighter." And as the southern plantation owners would have gladly told you, "One man's slave owner is another man's caretaker."

In fact, modern Muslims are in very much the same position as American Christians before the Civil War. Slave owners and their allies used the Bible's clear and indisputable acceptance of slavery to construct a theology of Christian slavery. They made strong, Scripture-based arguments that slavery not only was acceptable but was, indeed, God's will.

In America, this corrupt appeal to religion over justice didn't work. The argument over slavery was settled at Appomattox, not at divinity school. But the antislavery argument kept Christianity on the side of righteousness, rather than let it become hijacked by self-interested extremists. Will modern Islamists step forward to wage a similar fight?

If not, then their rednecks will win, too.

11

Mario Brothers

Mario Savio, where are you when we need you?

Where is the "eloquent, disheveled philosophy student" who, according to the *San Francisco Chronicle,* "kicked off the fiery Free Speech Movement at the University of California at Berkeley" in November 1964?

It could be argued that Mario Savio won the civil rights battle of the 1960s single-handedly. Standing atop a police squad car in Berkeley, unsteady in his stocking feet, urging students to "fight the power," Savio became the symbol of the most fundamental of the civil rights over which America struggled: free speech.

And once speech—ideas, arguments, intellectual confrontation—became the battleground, the Old South was doomed to defeat.

And, oh my, how Mr. Savio must have appeared to Southerners hunched over their corn bread and collard greens watching Walter Cronkite on their black-and-white TVs, sending a shudder through every white southern father with a daughter in a co-ed college.

There were no Mario Savios down South because Southerners have never cared much for the notion of freedom of expression. As a southern friend once told me when I played the "free speech" card during an argument, "Michael, you got the right to say whatever you want as long as you keep it to yourself."

Free speech and good manners are irreconcilable values: Talk long enough and somebody's gonna get hurt. So most civilized southern households live by the dictum "If you can't say something nice, shut up and drink."

Then again, as a Southerner who never learned either to shut up or hold my liquor, I frequently ran into that other edict of southern conversation: "I may not like what you say, but I will defend with my life the right to give you an ass whoopin' if you open your big fat mouth one more time."

Believe me, I know. I was banned from the South Carolina public radio network for making fun of the state legislature. Banned, as in "forbidden to appear; silenced; censored by the government." Only in the South, right?

What annoyed me is that I had done nothing wrong. My (unpaid) job at the time was to provide humorous commentary each week for one of the insufferably humorless programs on our government-run radio network. Each week I wrote a commentary, submitted the script for approval, recorded the approved text, and handed it over to be edited yet again.

One week my comments focused on a new ethics bill just approved by the General Assembly, a body that featured, at the time, at least one felon convicted of election fraud. Any ethics bill he could support had to be top-notch, I opined, and besides: "South Carolinians don't care about ethics in government. Bar all criminals from the state legislature, and there won't be enough members left to convene a quorum, much less provide the entertaining election scandals to which we've become accustomed."

I wrote it, they reviewed it, they edited it, and they broadcast it. And then the South Carolina Educational Radio Network banned *me*.

That's when I found out it's not public radio, it's *government* radio. You know . . . like Pravda?

Fascinatingly there was not the least hint of embarrassment that a phone call from a legislator could shut up a critic of the government. There was unanimity of agreement, even from my friends and family, that the incident was entirely my fault. "If you want the government to pay you to insult them," my fellow Southerners told me, "move to New York and apply for an NEA grant."

None of my southern friends were particularly upset that I had been the victim of censorship because (a) I'm a smart-ass who had it coming and (b) stifling dissent is as southern as grits and redeye gravy.

During the Revolutionary War, Southerners were the most pro-Tory of the colonists, and many southern patriots were happy to keep their mouths shut in exchange for a promise from the British to leave them alone. Loudmouthed agitators were unwelcome. A visit from Samuel Adams would have been as warmly received by Tory Southerners as a visit from the pope.

During the slave years, Southerners who spoke out against slavery were under constant pressure to keep quiet or migrate North. Pro-abolition newspapers were confiscated, burned out, or worse. After southern forces fired on Fort Sumter, even longtime Southerners who supported slavery but opposed the Civil War were forced to flee.

In the Jim Crow South, silence was essential to maintaining the status quo. People engaged in demonstrably irrational and indefensible behavior are easily distracted. As soon as someone asks a reasonable question—"Hey, why is it that a black doctor isn't allowed to vote, but Virgil, the guy who sticks refrigerator magnets to the plate in his head, is our new legislator?"—it becomes tempting to give a reasonable answer. And the one thing the South could never withstand is reason.

That's why every Southerner defending some indefensible aspect of life in the South keeps the admonition, "Well, if you don't like it, why don't you just leave?" tucked away like a knife in his boot. This is obviously not an argument, but rather a rejection of the idea of arguing. However, it brings the desired solution of less speech.

This was the greatest gulf between me and my southern homeland. Of course, people should speak out, it seemed to me, especially people who are challenging us and saying things we don't want to hear. A place that allows free and open dissent, like the North, is an inherently better place than a society that suppresses it. I would pull my hair and gurgle in frustration every time another Confederate knothead growled at me, "Wuhl, Michael, I-95 has two lanes innit, and one's always headin' North. If you don' lahk it here, you kin jes leave."

Aaarrggh! Do you really think that if I leave, you suddenly *won't* be stupid anymore?

"I dunno," would come the answer, "but it's worth a try . . ."

Civil rights activists coming South to confront the laws

and customs of the 1950s and '60s ran straight into this southern stone wall of silence in the cause of stupidity. Rednecks, reactionaries, law-and-orderers, and love-it-or-leave-it types rarely offered overt, rational defenses of segregation or the denial of basic civil rights. In the South, debates in favor of discrimination were few. Arguments about why you ought to climb your Yankee ass back on the bus and go home were far more common.

But by the late 1960s, the days of telling people to "shut up and mind your own business" were over. Not only could you not suppress speech about race, politics, etc.—after the Free Speech Movement, it became wrong even to try. The southern value of polite silence was gone, trumped by the new value of free speech and confrontation.

The symbol of these new freedoms appeared in stocking feet on the hood of a Berkeley police car and on millions of TV sets across the South.

The North had won.

And so thirty years later, Mario Savio returned in triumph to Berkeley and celebrated the anniversary of the Free Speech Movement. He was there to remind America how much things had changed since 1964, how the progressive vision of ever-expanding freedom had conquered the political forces of silence and intimidation. The five-day commemoration, in early December 1994, featured "poetry readings, films, panels, rallies, a colloquium, a dance," and, according to the University of California's website, "a hootenanny."

The only thing missing from Berkeley that day was free speech.

On the very day that Mario returned to Berkeley to celebrate the freedom to dissent, three Berkeley residents were under assault from the federal Department of Housing and Urban Development . . . for speaking. Three local citizens who had complained about a government housing project were facing $100,000 in fines and an ongoing investigation that would end, they were told, only if they would agree to stop complaining about the HUD development in Berkeley.

Berkeley, California, whose new motto is "Shut Up or Else."

Berkeley—where just six weeks earlier, wacko Holocaust-revisionist historian David Irving was forced to cancel a speech because the school couldn't guarantee his safety in the face of liberal protests. Irving was forced to an off-campus site, where his book tables were overturned and his property destroyed by Berkeleyites celebrating their free speech traditions.

Berkeley—where in 2001, students stormed the campus newspaper and looted the paper boxes in protest of a paid advertisement. The editor of the *Daily Californian* showed his dedication to free speech and a free press by groveling before the protesters and apologizing for printing an unpopular opinion.

Berkeley—where the number of scheduled campus public speakers who have been disinvited or shouted down by students and faculty members is well into double digits, including former Israeli prime minister Benjamin Netanyahu, conservative organizer Daniel Flynn, U.N. delegate Jeanne Kirkpatrick, and former Berkeley-alum-turned-conservative-carnival-barker David Horowitz.

You know—Berkeley: home of the Free Speech (for people we like) Movement!

Mario Savio died in 1996, and his obituary in the *San Francisco Chronicle* contained a sharply ironic bit of unintentional humor: "Savio's 24-year-old friend Jack Weinberg had violated a campus rule that seems farfetched by today's standards—a ban against on-campus politics. Weinberg had set up a leafleting table on the plaza on behalf of a civil rights group."

Getting in trouble for speaking out on politics at Berkeley is "farfetched"? Where has this obit writer been living? In Mario's lifetime, Berkeley morphed from the fire wall of free speech to the ivory-towered headquarters of the new P.C. speech police.

All through the Civil Rights Movement, southern communities tried to keep "outside agitators" from having access to the public arena, from applying their First Amendment rights to assemble and speak. But somehow it wasn't as embarrassing to see the right to free speech rejected by poorly educated goobers cracking wise about "Martin Luther Koon." They were idiots—they weren't expected to know any better. But to see free speech rejected at Berkeley—not once or twice, but again and again as a fundamental shift in values—proves how redneck our nation has become. The old Northern ideal that free expression is a value in and of itself, that allowing unpopular, even disturbing ideas to be expressed is a good thing—this ideal is lost. Instead, we've gone back to the southern standard: If you're going to say something that might upset people, don't. Better still, let us shut your mouth for you.

When Jeanne Kirkpatrick was banned from speaking

at Berkeley, students weren't the only people slamming the door on freedom of expression. Some faculty members also argued that letting her express her opinions wasn't necessarily a good thing. At the University of Chicago, Professor Cass Sunstein leads an intellectual movement among liberals who argue that freedom to say things people don't like (especially people like Cass Sunstein) is probably too much freedom.

Doesn't anyone remember when "lib"-er-als used to believe in "lib"-er-ty? Does anyone see the eerie similarities of angry white segregationists shouting down civil rights protesters and ripping up their fliers, and foamy-mouthed Berkeley beer-hall Marxists shouting down conservatives and kicking over their book tables?

Alas, it was the San Francisco HUD offices under the Clinton administration—not Nixon's—that used threats to silence outspoken citizens. The Berkeley Three, as they came to be known, were locals unhappy about a local HUD decision, and they were doing exactly what you'd expect Berkeley types to do: writing letters, speaking out at meetings, attending public forums, smoking pot . . . Part of this is conjecture, of course.

Anyway, the San Francisco office determined that merely complaining about HUD's activities was in and of itself a violation of the Fair Housing Act. After first threatening the Berkeley Three with large fines and lengthy litigation, the oily folks at HUD then offered a deal: HUD would end the investigation and drop the fines if the three residents just agreed to cease all litigation and stop publishing articles and fliers against the project.

How nice.

After five years of legal wrangling, the voice of reason

was finally heard. U.S. District Judge Marilyn Hall Patel stepped in and lifted the Democratic administration's jackboot off the protesters' larynx. She said that HUD's actions "chilled [their] right to free speech and the right to petition the government for a redress of grievances. . . . Any reasonable official in your position would have recognized the constitutional impropriety of investigating purely expressive activity."

Oh, came HUD's reply, we're supposed to be *reasonable*?

It is safe to say that in the twenty-first century, Berkeley has become all but synonymous with the suppression of free speech and the so-called P.C. movement. Too bad that "politically correct" has become such an innocuous phrase, because there's a powerful, repugnant bit of redneck thinkology cloaked within it.

The "fight the power" fascists at Berkeley aren't total idiots. They understand that they're abusing a fundamental freedom when they keep their political opponents from speaking. How do they defend this obviously bad behavior? By trumping the need for freedom of expression with a more pressing need, like maintaining good order, or keeping hurtful words from causing others pain, or nurturing a political system under assault. If these arguments sound familiar, you're probably from the South, for they're exactly what pro-segregation editorialists offered in defense of suppressing dissent during the civil rights era.

How many towns banned, or attempted to ban, Dr. King or the Freedom Riders from their borders? How many southern judges were asked to overrule free speech in favor of safe streets?

During the civil rights era, many cities argued that the opinions expressed by some controversial figures were just too dangerous to be allowed in their communities. Southerners didn't want to hear what the civil rights activists were saying, and, it was argued, the outside agitators had nothing to say worth hearing, anyway.

Thirty years later, a black Charleston, South Carolina, city councilman proposed a similar ordinance barring all "hate groups" (as defined by the city government) from assembling or speaking in Charleston. "The people of Charleston don't want to hear from those groups," he insisted, echoing the sentiment of the white city leaders who would have banned his father's public protests a generation earlier.

Maintaining good order is one long-standing southern value often invoked to override questions of free speech. Another is the need to be pleasant, and when it comes to southern hospitality at the expense of free speech, the Confederistas have nothing on St. Paul, Minnesota.

The people of St. Paul enacted a law making it a crime to say anything that "arouses anger, alarm or resentment in others on the basis of race, color, creed, religion or gender," thereby criminalizing the Klan, the Black Panthers, the Shriners, the Christian Coalition, Pat Buchanan, Alan Dershowitz, the National Organization for Women, the NEA, and virtually every sketch performed on *Saturday Night Live,* along with one or two episodes of *The Brady Bunch.*

Were this law truly enforced, every comedy club would be shuttered, every politician gagged and every talk radio microphone impounded. What kind of idiot thought this was a good idea?

Well, a majority of the citizens of St. Paul, for starters. This idea wasn't foisted on the populace; it was very popular among the citizenry, the vast majority of whom, I must point out, are not Southerners. St. Paul is pink with the smiling, well-fed faces of liberals, lefties, and other usual suspects of America's northern political tradition.

And as good, modern American liberals, they absolutely do not believe in the First Amendment.

Passing a law against impolite speech is the kind of reactionary lawmaking traditionally associated with rural outposts in the Ozark Mountains. It smacks of the days when the state of Arkansas passed a legislative request that H. L. Mencken be deported for insulting the honor of their state in print. After one devastatingly accurate portrait of their homeland in the 1920s, Arkansas legislators took the floor to demand that "the dirty Jew" Mencken be sent to his home country at once. And if Mencken had actually been Jewish and hadn't been born in Baltimore, they might have succeeded.

It is now widely agreed that the Arkansans were asses . . . so what, pray tell, are the St. Paulines? The folks of Arkansas only tried to silence one man, while the people of St. Paul criminalized all speech that arouses "anger, alarm or resentment."

What's particularly southern about St. Paul's approach to free speech is that it was focused on the *reaction* to the words, not the words themselves. If I were a citizen of St. Paul and someone began intoning the Lord's Prayer outside my bedroom window, I could reasonably assert that I was alarmed—he might be a bomb-toting anti-abortionist or a televangelist with a runaway libido. I could furthermore reasonably claim resentment of the

King James Version of the Bible, which with its soaring poetry exposed the limited vocabulary of my public school education or the comparatively lifeless prose of my Scientology pamphlets.

The purpose of the ordinance, in other words, was not to stop the transmission of the ideas but to protect the delicate sensibilities of the hearer. Is free speech really worth letting folks get upset over? Why don't you just sit down and have a julep—you'll feel better.

The St. Paul censorship code was so clearly unconstitutional that even some members of the U.S. Supreme Court noticed, and it was overturned. But fear not, Redneck Nation, for the fight against free speech continues, and with an unusual ally: the ACLU.

FOOTLOOSE WITH THE FIRST AMENDMENT

If you've seen the movie *Footloose,* you have my sympathy. But you probably recall how ridiculous the premise was: an American town in the modern era where rock music and dancing were banned and teenagers actually paid attention to sermons on sinful music preached by a balding, middle-aged pastor. The film is unwatchable for many reasons, not the least of which is that it's simply impossible in these modern times to imagine such a place in America.

Well, if *Footloose* seems beyond the pale, what to make of a state with a list of banned words, words you cannot speak publicly at work to any person for any reason. Does it sound crazy? Does it sound ridiculous? Does it sound like . . . California?

In one of the most bizarre judicial rulings ever, the California State Supreme Court voted 4–3 to establish a list of banned words. The ruling was the result of a lawsuit brought by a group of Hispanic workers claiming that their boss used racist slurs and comments when talking to them. In upholding the damages, the court barred "any future use of a list of offensive words in the workplace—even outside the presence of the [Latino employees] and even if welcome or overtly permitted."

Worse, the ACLU, whose attitude toward our liberties is getting less civil every day, supported this overt, obvious, and intentional violation of First Amendment freedoms. As civil libertarian Nat Hentoff noted at the time, "the ACLU of Northern California submitted an amicus brief in enthusiastic support of this prior restraint of speech. . . . [The ACLU] has now allowed itself to be gleefully cited by its opponents as agreeing that certain words can no longer be spoken in certain places before there is clear evidence that any of those words has created discrimination in a particular instance or in a particular context."

Making fun of the Old South for policing water fountains and checking who sat in which bus seat is easy. But it's also history. Right now the state of California has speech police patrolling workbenches and factory floors, listening for the "forbidden words"—a real-life parody of an old George Carlin routine.

If you think I'm exaggerating about the speech police, you might want to chat with Janice Barton of Manistee, Michigan. The speech police didn't just catch her, they sentenced her to forty-five days in jail. According to the *Manistee Chronicle*, Barton was arrested, tried, and convicted of the crime of telling her mother in a one-on-one conversation that "spics," as she put it, ought to learn to speak English. Now, this is hardly a noble sentiment, but is it a crime?

The comment, spoken in a crowded restaurant, was overheard by an off-duty deputy sheriff who took down Barton's license plate when she left. In October 1998, Barton was charged with violating a city ordinance against "insulting conduct in a public place." The actual law reads like it was written by my grandmother to be read immediately before Sunday dinner. "No person shall engage in any indecent, insulting, immoral or obscene conduct in any public place." And clean your plate, too.

Towns all over Michigan have nearly identical laws, it should be noted. It should be further noted that all of these incidents of outrageous limits on personal liberty are occurring in the very heart of traditional American Northernism.

California, Minnesota, Michigan—these are all bastions of progressivism, leaders in what we Southerners viewed as Yankee agitation. These stories are not isolated incidents from oddball locales like Ottumwa, Iowa, or Moose River, Maine. Cass Sunstein is a prominent member of the University of Chicago's law school, where he wrote *Democracy and the PROBLEM of Free Speech* (emphasis added). His rejection of free speech as a near-absolute right was well received, not by far-right proto-Nazis, but by his northern liberal allies who nearly all agree that as long as Rush Limbaugh makes more money than they do, there is too much free speech in America.

The inevitable—in fact, the only—counterargument those who abandon free speech offer is that some speech is too vile to be allowed. Racist taunts, screams of hateful anger, the music of Celine Dion—what value do these expressions truly have, and what about all the harm they cause?

But even if we could agree that some expressions of free speech are too much for a society to bear, who gets to decide which ones they are? Inevitably it's the government that will decide, and these governments (as Mario Savio would surely tell you) cannot be trusted. Imagine how happy George Wallace and Bull Connor would have been to have the power to suppress "hate-filled speech" attacking the good Christian folk of the South and the honor of their heritage. They would have been more than happy to distribute their list of "banned words" to every civil rights gathering in their home states.

"Ah, but, Michael, that's the mistake you make with this Redneck Nation nonsense. Northerners don't abuse power that way. We Yankees wouldn't suppress political speech or outlaw dissent. We truly are different from those Southerners you compare us with. That stuff might have happened in Wilmington, North Carolina, but it wouldn't in Waukesha, Wisconsin."

Oh, really? From wire reports:

Waukesha County, Wisconsin, Sued for Park Ordinance Prohibiting Free Speech

MILWAUKEE—Robert Thompson, a resident of Waukesha County, Wisconsin, filed a lawsuit challenging a county ordinance preventing him from passing out copies of The Bible and the U.S. Constitution in county parks.

Waukesha County Ordinance Chapter 20 pro-
hibits public discussions on religion or politics
within the county parks unless a written permit
from the county park and planning commission has
first been granted. . . . *The ordinance contains a flat
ban on religious or political literature distribution
in public parks* [emphasis added]. Violating the ordinance can result in fines and up to 90 days in jail.

This law, a direct, frontal assault on political speech, was
the law of the land in an American city in 1999. Not 1899,
but on the cusp of the twenty-first century, and in a solid
northern community in a solidly liberal state. Such a law
in a southern county in 1969 would have been viewed as
proof of the oppression and backwardness of the South.
How, my Yankee friend, should we view it today?

Once the law was challenged, the good folks of
Waukesha quickly saw they had a court case they
couldn't win and withdrew. It is safe to assume, however,
that similar laws still exist, and it is safer still to assume
they'll be found north—not south—of the Mason-Dixon
line. For that is the ultimate irony of all of these sad stories of modern redneckery: You already knew it.

As soon as you began reading this chapter about free
speech, you knew what was coming. There are dozens—
no, hundreds—of these stories, and they all involve
places like Berkeley and St. Paul and Chicago and Seattle, and they all confirm that the modern enemy of free
speech is comprised almost entirely of its old champions
from the civil rights era.

If I say "racism," you still say "South." If I say "illiterate," you still say "South." But if the word association is

"censorship," the natural choice is "North." When the next Mario Savio appears, he will no doubt return to Berkeley to fight for the cause of free speech.

This time, I doubt he'll make it out alive.

12

Submit, Hell!

*Radical feminists are hard to find in the South; the great
majority of females are not in sympathy with lesbianism; they
do not generally dispense with their undergarments or go out in
public without their make-up. Furthermore, they reject the
notion of an all-encompassing cross-cultural and historical
patriarchal plot to subjugate women. If in fact such a plot ever
existed, many southern women have been all-too-willing
accomplices.*

—Margaret Ripley Wolfe, Daughters of Canaan:
A Saga of Southern Women

*A wife is to submit herself graciously to the servant leadership of
her husband even as the church willingly submits to the
headship of Christ.*

—From the mission statement of the
Southern Baptist Convention

*I am not sitting here standing by my man like Tammy Wynette.
I am sitting here because I love and respect him.*

—Hillary Rodham Clinton, with her husband, on *60 Minutes*

t was the Tammy Wynette line that really hurt.

Every northern woman knows what a "Tammy Wynette" is—that downtrodden southern damsel trudging through Sam's Wholesale Club, a squirming toddler over her hip and a dark bruise under her eye. She's the one trying to scrape together a week's worth of groceries from what's left after paying the tab for her husband's weekend drinking and his unexplained credit card charges from a local motel. A "Tammy Wynette" is a helpless female, a perpetual victim, an unenlightened sister who has yet to add the word "empowered" to her vocabulary.

This was the type of woman—the powerless, dependent, prototypically *southern* woman—that then-Mrs. Clinton denied being. She couched her denial in this language because she knew it would resonate with women from Boston to the San Francisco Bay.

Working in politics as I have, I've had the opportunity to hear the way southern women, particularly the low-income and/or religious women, are viewed by their northern sisters. Listening to northeastern liberals, one would think southern gals spend their days clad in burkas awaiting their next caning. I remember listening to a conversation in Westchester County, New York, in which a liberal, pro-abortion Republican was talking about her pro-life southern counterparts, and I couldn't tell if she thought they were victims of brainwashing or Vichy-style traitors to the feminist cause. After a particularly heated rant about "telling me what to do with my body" and the lack of government-subsidized day care, she declared, "We wouldn't put up with that up here."

And there it is: what southern women will put up with. Those poor, demure damsels, oppressed by southern culture, utterly lacking in empowerment and unable to sing the "I Am Woman" anthem of the northern sisterhood. We've got to get these women a subscription to *Cosmo* and access to the Oxygen channel—stat!

In northern eyes, there are two kinds of southern women: If they're attractive and affluent, they're vapid, sorority-girl sellouts with big hair and bigger smiles, hanging off the arm of old money or nouveau riche manhood. If they're poor and pudgy, they're political prisoners of the trailer park plantation, spending their days with Judge Judy and their nights with Miss Cleo.

And either way, they're much too fond of Elvis.

The defining characteristic of these redneck women is the relationship they have with men. Southern women, so the assumption goes, are either helpless damsels, delicate and genteel, wholly dependent upon men for protection, or they are trailer trash, desperate Paula Joneses who will put themselves through whatever humiliations are required to hold on to their wayward men. A stereotypical southern woman either needs a man to rescue her or needs to be rescued from her man—depending on her economic status.

I find the northern female's contempt for the southern belle's perceived weaknesses deliciously ironic, coming as it does from a group of women who lack the strength to protect themselves from so much as an auto shop girlie calendar, an off-color joke, or (as will be demonstrated) the works of Goya. If you are looking for erudite, academically minded women, then the South will be slim pickin's, I concede. But if you're looking for strong, powerful women who have taught their men to answer "How high?" when they say "Jump!" you gotta be whistlin' Dixie.

WHERE THE GIRLS ARE

I learned about southern womanhood the hard way, from broken hearts and sore backsides endured during a misspent youth devoted to their pursuit and capture. There was Laurie, a blonde with a soft southern accent so smooth you could spread it on a biscuit, who moved away and left me crushed in the fourth grade.

There was Georgia, a dark brunet whose every furtive classroom glance my senior year told me, "Not if you were the last breathing biped on planet Earth, Graham."

There was Wendy, a singer, an actress, a beauty pageant contestant, and the queen of her corner of Lexington County, South Carolina. She was perhaps the last woman in America to be "courted" rather than dated, and Wendy's father sometimes took a system of valet parking to handle the crush of suitors awaiting an audience.

Christine was the embodiment of southern femininity: graceful, demure, and drop-dead gorgeous. We met at a state high school band event, where she stole my heart. When I drove ninety minutes to North Augusta, to reclaim it, I was greeted by the embodiment of southern fatherhood: imposing, inarticulate, and well armed.

In college, I dated a few women from up North, but the cultural chasm could not be bridged; not by love, or even the amazing thing that one girl did with the cherry stem and the handcuffs. And so today, after minor mistakes, major disasters, and one near-death experience, I have fulfilled my destiny as the husband of a true daughter of the Confederacy: my lovely bride, the Warden.

If you have to ask why I call her the Warden, you know nothing of the species of womanhood indigenous to the South. And the Warden is a Southerner, through and through. Born in Bennettsville, South Carolina (her mother was "Miss Bennettsville High School", the Warden grew up an only child—taking piano, riding horses, and learning the biblical command that husbands should love their wives as Christ loved the church: He does all the suffering, while She builds lavish, ornate buildings, dresses in expensive clothes, and advocates celibacy.

The Warden grew up Catholic in South Carolina, a state where the term "papist plot" is still used at appropriate public gatherings. I met her at a Christian coffeehouse when we were both in high school, and we dated for a short time before she dumped me (of course). Nearly ten years later, we had a happenstance reunion. She was working as a newspaper reporter and driving a black Corvette with T-tops and a vanity plate that read "Blondi."

I never had a chance.

I do not claim to be an expert on southern women. As a man, I can't honestly claim to understand any woman, including my wife, my mother, or even my seven-year-old daughter. But I can report from my personal experience as a tireless observer of the local wildlife that there are just two kinds of southern women: the kind who will kick your ass and the kind who will get their Daddy to do it for them.

Either way, you lose.

My grandmother Graham is the strongest, most fearless woman I've ever known. Once, while picking butter beans, she killed a rattlesnake using just an empty grape Nehi bottle (something about the shape, I'm told; apparently it won't work with a Dr Pepper). She was in her sixties at the time.

Her daughter, my aunt Lib, rid herself and her two daughters of a loser husband and father through the effective brandishing of a firearm. No shots were fired, no charges filed, and no appeals sought. He took the truck in the driveway and the clothes on his back and, at last report, considered himself well treated.

Lib's sister, Celie, lived for many years in a cabin back in the dense woods of a thousand-acre hunting club. The waters were filled with snakes, the woods alive with carnivores of all shapes and sizes, and yet it was nothing for her husband to go and leave her and the three young boys for days at a time as he took care of business.

These are not weak women jumping up on the dining table at the first sign of danger and waiting for a man to come to the rescue. Maybe it's a reflection on their low opinion of southern manhood, but southern women don't seem to expect much from us in the first place.

As for the intellectual capacity of the typical southern woman, I cannot praise it as inordinately large because (a) she's a Southerner and (b) worse, she's an American. And I'm not going to pretend that there isn't a political and social conservatism at her core that would discomfit the average feminist, liberal, progressive, or Victorian. But I cannot allow the denigration of the strength and independence of southern women to go unchallenged.

If you really want to find insecure women dependent upon men, you can skip Blanche DuBois and Melanie Wilkes. You won't find her down South anymore. At least, not since she left Arkansas.

Aye, there's the rub: Hillary Clinton (née Rodham)—the acme of American feminism, idolized by the establishment media as the fullness of self-realized womanhood itself—is seen by Southerners for what she truly is: pure redneck.

Hillary Rodham is the least empowered political woman since Marie Antoinette.

From her law firm partnership in Arkansas to her U.S. Senate seat in New York to the "Property of the White House" ashtrays on the unintentionally donated coffee table in her Georgetown apartment, Senator Rodham owes everything—*everything*—she has to her husband, to her man. Whenever she displayed her barely concealed contempt for women who "have stayed home and baked cookies and had teas," southern women stood at a hot sink of dishes and rolled their eyes.

First of all, if Senator Rodham had been a true southern lady, she would have sat politely next to her husband on television that Super Bowl Sunday night and then filled the fireplace with the remains of his personal belongings on her way out the door Monday morning. I have personal knowledge of what it is like to wrong a southern woman, and it doesn't involve loving pats on your arm while you humiliate her on national television. The only thing a real southern woman would be patting lovingly is the butt end of her Smith & Wesson.

I'm not suggesting that Senator Rodham should have done anything to violate the Homeland Security Act, but if she truly is, as advertised, the incarnation of modern feminism, feminists are a particularly uninspiring lot. It's undeniable that there are southern women who stand by their man though he's hurt and humiliated them time and time again. And there is certainly a strain of insecure southern female that won't walk away from a bad man or a worse beating.

Of course, these women exist down South: They're called rednecks! It is highly significant that the woman who trudged through Gennifer and Kathleen and Monica and Juanita, and dragged her daughter along, is still regarded with pride by the contemporary feminist movement. She remained until the end of her husband's term of office one of America's most admired women, even as the Secret Service was stopping her at the White House door to search her for spoons.

Standin' by her cheatin' husband, throwing lamps within earshot of the neighbors, taking the towels at checkout, and then using her husband's good-ol'-boy connections to get her a job—Senator Rodham does everything a redneck man would want except dip snuff and cook 'shine. So how did she get to be an American feminist icon?

GONE WITH THE WIND

If the classic southern woman is sensitive, frail, and ever vulnerable to the waywardness of men, then the American feminist movement has migrated en masse onto the Tara plantation. Modern feminists are the most delicate flowers of our society, ever vulnerable to the slightest change in barometric pressure. Consider these examples:

• A professor of women's studies at Penn State demands that a print of Goya's *The Naked Maja* be removed from her classroom because it creates a hostile work environment, making it impossible for her to empower her female students. "Any nude picture of a female encourages males to make remarks about body parts," she said.

• A law professor at Northwestern University urged the criminalization of catcalls and other harassing comments made toward women on public streets, asking that such speech be legally punishable as "assaultive behavior." The goal, apparently, is to protect frail women from the destructive power of whistling.

• Years before Attorney General John Ashcroft ordered drapes to cover the topless statues of the Justice Department, female workers in the Vermont state office building complained that they were being sexually harassed by a mural of Christopher Columbus arriving in the New World. The painting, which showed topless native women greeting the white European males, had to be covered with a bedsheet for the protection of Vermont's womanhood.

• When animal-rights activists at UC Santa Barbara announced that all pets should be referred to as "companion animals," a professor wondered aloud whether that meant the centerfolds in *Penthouse* magazine would now be known as "Penthouse Companion Animals" instead of "pets." Fifteen college-educated women filed sexual harassment charges against him for unauthorized use of humor.

• Professor Mary P. Koss of the University of Arizona authored "The Scope of Rape," a survey of college-aged women which, she says, indicates that one in four has been the victim of rape or attempted rape. She includes in that number, however, women who consented to sex but had been drinking. These women, she believes, are the victims of rape. "The law punishes the drunk driver who kills a pedestrian," she argues. "And likewise, the law needs to be there to protect the drunk woman from the driver of the penis."

Now, when it comes to sex, I'm certainly no Wilt Chamberlain, but I've driven around the block once or twice. And, as a product of the rural South, I find this last item the most confusing and offensive. Professor Koss considers herself a feminist. She's struggling against the patriarchal attitudes of a society that considers women emotional, irrational, and unstable. And what is her argument regarding sexual harassment and rape?

That women can't hold their liquor.

Obviously it is possible for a drunk woman to be raped. But that is not what the sexual harassment harpies terrorizing American society are talking about. They want men to protect women from themselves, to play daddy to their drunken dates and lovingly tuck them, unmussed, into their beds. And, men, if you don't, if you treat your date like a rational human being who decides to drink, date, and do the nasty like a grown-up, your friendly, local feminists will throw you into jail.

Once again, I know women who believe men are just naturally stronger and more disciplined than the fairer sex. I know women who expect men to take care of them when they can't take care of themselves. But I didn't know these women were *feminists*. I thought they were Southern Baptists.

And while we're on the subject of sexual entanglements, ladies, *THERE IS NO SUCH THING AS DATE RAPE!* Stop saying it! You sound like some loopy cast member from an uncensored performance of *The Vagina Monologues*.

There is rape—sex by force and against your will. And then there is sex—either explicitly consensual or with no demonstrated objections. What else is there? What category is missing?

Ladies, if you're on a date with a good friend you've known for years, and the guy uses physical force to overcome your objections and violate you, it's rape. Period. And if you meet a total stranger in a parking lot and, overcome with passion, allow him to explore your nether regions without complaint, it wasn't rape, it was sex. That's it.

What is the scenario for "date rape"? It's either rape or not rape. You know what date rape is? Date rape is the mournful cry of a woman who suddenly realizes she just slept with a loser.

In an attempt to prevent this confusion, some northern colleges have begun to quantify the art of romance. One such school, Antioch College in Yellow Springs, Ohio, has made a name for itself through its sexual contact policies. At Antioch, students who are seeking intimacy (for the most part, men) must get explicit, stated permission from their partners (for the most part, women) before they take any actions. Want to neck? Ask first: "May I please slide my tongue down your throat?"

Want to cop a feel? "May I please check the freshness of your fulsome loaves?"

Want to, well, you know . . . "May I please mount you like a stallion and cry, 'On, Thunder King, on!'?"

How romantic it must be on a warm, moonlit night to stroll the campus of Antioch and hear the sounds of spring: the evening breeze, the rustling leaves, and the extended contract negotiations as a young man (hereafter known as the Party of the First Part) pitches woo to his lady love (a.k.a. the Plantiff).

Some liberal feminists even label consensual sex "rape" if the man pressures the woman verbally. Verbal pressuring is when a guy seeks sex by, say, threatening to break off the relationship or (my usual dating strategy) falling to his knees and begging for it. This is psychological coercion and is no different from a knife to the throat or a gun to the head, feminists argue. Men engaged in this coercion should be punished appropriately.

So let me get this straight: Women can do anything men can do, except say no? Are modern, postfeminist women truly so weak, so defenseless, so utterly dependent upon the kindness of lovers? Then they have all turned into Daddy's Girls, those petite flowers of my southern youth whose chastity was ever guarded by their proper upbringing, their commitment to Christ, and the certain justice of their father's twelve-gauge. Only this feminist incarnation of the southern belle relies, not on Big Daddy, but on Uncle Sam. They have loaded up the legal system with layer upon layer of gender-specific protections, court-supported petticoats to cover their inbred feminine frailty.

How else to explain why simple speech and innocuous images are seen as predatory members of some sexual harassment conspiracy? The Goya and the Columbus mural mentioned earlier are hardly exceptions. In Dayton, Ohio, it was Titian's *Venus of Urbino* that was vandalized and eventually removed because feminists "felt they were being sexually harassed by the painting." At the University of Nebraska, a graduate student was forced to remove a photo of his own wife from his desk because she was wearing a bikini and some of his coworkers felt harassed.

The same women who roll their eyes at the affectations of our grandmothers—like using euphemisms for "breast" and "leg" in the presence of fried chicken—find the works of Michelangelo too offensive to be viewed in mixed company.

Are the new American feminists puritans, prudes, or just pathetic examples of powerlessness? These women remind me of the Oral Roberts University students I traveled to Europe with my senior year. I was the student conductor of the concert choir and we toured the continent, performing at Notre Dame, and St. Peter's in Rome. In Florence, the must-see location was the Galleria dell' Accademia and Michelangelo's *David*.

My previous exposure to visual arts had been largely limited to black velvet paintings featuring canine card players, but the *David* absolutely mesmerized me. To see it, you must work your way through long halls at the gallery filled with lesser works by Michelangelo, works that prepare you, step by step, to see his ultimate masterpiece.

Then you enter the main hall and there it is: the fulfillment of all human potential realized before your eyes in carved stone. Michelangelo's *David* is the reason I don't believe in angels. It is visual proof that humans may achieve the divine.

I went to see the *David* with thirty or so other ORU students, among them three classically southern, nonfeminist females who entered the main hall about the same time I did. As I gazed, openmouthed and moist-eyed at what I believe to be the greatest work of visual art ever crafted by human hands, I couldn't help noticing these girls, clumped together and giggling uncomfortably.

"What's their problem?" my mind wondered. Why weren't they stunned, stammering, and amazed? Then I realized: David is nude. Nakkie. Here is the towering image of the majesty of humankind, but these tender Christian girls with their mega-church delicacy cannot look upon it because you can see his pee-pee.

I tried to ignore them, to reenter the internal mists of euphoria the *David* inspires, but I couldn't. I had let them ruin the moment.

Finally I stomped over to them and in a whispered shout asked, "Okay, so if I hang a hat on it . . . *then* can you look?" They scampered red-faced to the gift shop, never to return.

There is no difference between these cowering college girls intimidated by the marble manhood of David and the doctor of gender studies screeching from under her desk that somebody better get the latest Hooter's Girls calendar out of the janitor's closet before she calls the cops. I take it back—there is a difference. The feminists have a self-righteous sense that they're stronger and more independent than my ORU friends. But in fact, they're just another bunch of rednecks. They just have better résumés.

THE OTHER WOMAN

What the new feminist woman lacks in courage, however, she makes up in libido. That is my conclusion after watching a few episodes of HBO's *Sex and the City*.

The first time I watched the show, I experienced a vague feeling of déjà vu. The show celebrates the total, uninhibited balls-to-the-wall pursuit of sex by four women in New York. The most popular character is Samantha Jones, played by Kim Cattrall, on whom I've had a low-grade crush since her star turn as Lassie in *Porky's*.

Samantha is the most talked-about character on this

very popular show because her sexuality has no limits. Every episode features a "What fetish will she flirt with this week?" subplot for Samantha. Straight sex, lesbian sex, machine-operated sex, multiple-partner sex, there was even some talk of cross-species interaction, but, as of this writing, HBO has yet to figure out how to get it past the folks at PETA.

Enlightened, urbane American women absolutely love this show. They are obsessed with these women, who, in turn, are obsessed in each episode with men: getting them, pleasing them, and, most important, being pleased by them in ever more exotic ways. If these four women think about anything other than their naughty bits, they do so only off camera.

What was it about these women that struck me as familiar? I have never knowingly been in the presence of a nymphomaniac, and I have never known anyone, male or female, in such desperate need of a fashion rescue as Sarah Jessica Parker. Still, I kept thinking, I know these women from somewhere . . .

Of course! The mobile home ho's I knew in high school! How did Jim Carville put it? "Drag a hundred dollars through a trailer park and there's no telling what you'll find." What you'll find is the cast of *Sex and the City!*

Their escapades are ripped from the diaries of dirt-road, white-trash women who lurked along the edges of my social circles back in South Carolina. They weren't as affluent, attractive, or educated as Samantha and Carrie, but they operated on the same phallocentric principles as their city cousins. I would see them blowing past me on Harleys, their arms (almost) around the waists of their biker escorts; at roadhouse bars in West Columbia, South

Carolina, migrating around the pool tables from man to man—all the moves lateral ones. Where Samantha Jones might have a tag team with three lawyers in a Midtown hotel, she could be found wrasslin' the Shealy Brothers in the bunk of a big rig in the Flyin' C parking lot.

When asked about her character on *Sex and the City*, Cattrall says, "I don't consider her a slut, no. Slut has a negative connotation, and I don't think of anything that Samantha does as uninformed, not a joyous celebratory way of living." As a man of only modest morals, I say "Viva la celebración!" But a woman whose self-image is grounded in frequent sex with random partners in ever more contrived and uncomfortable positions is clearly a slut, whatever her other attributes. And it is just as clearly the case that if you took these same four women, stuck Confederate flag ball caps on their heads, and dropped them in a West Texas truck stop, they would be indistinguishable from the hardworking local gals.

It's not the open sexuality that makes the *Sex and the City* women rednecks, but rather the male-dependent trashiness, the willingness to go spelunking down the deepest, lowest crevices of our testosterone-driven fantasies. A woman who stands before Victorian society and shouts, "I defy your conventions and claim my body as my own!" is a feminist. A woman who lies down on the tailgate of a pickup truck and shouts, "The buffet's open, boys! Come and get it!" is, well, actually she's a girl I went to high school with.

Has it occurred to anyone else that the feminist icons of HBO are about as ideological as a meeting of the Republican Women's Club of Rocky Mount, North Carolina? If these women are advocating any ideas not already openly practiced by the ladies of the Junior League, it hasn't come to my attention. Samantha and Co. want sex, security, and some love, and they want them delivered to them by someone whose pants zip in the front. How did they become the new Freedom Riders of feminism?

Because the entire feminist movement has gone 'neck, that's how. Remember during the Lewinsky story, that parade of northern women proudly announcing that not only were they willing to overlook President Clinton's perjury and obstruction in a sexual harassment lawsuit but they would also be willing to orally service the man themselves in thanks for his solidly liberal politics. The Warden, who spent ten years with Knight-Ridder, nearly choked on her shrimp and grits when she read the following comment from former White House correspondent Nina Burleigh: "I'd be happy to give him a blow job just to thank him for keeping abortion legal."

An admiration for Ms. Burleigh's devotion to the cause of abortion rights doesn't dispel the low-rent, white-trash attitude behind the offer. Yes, I've known southern women who would "take a knee" in gratitude for services rendered, and, yes, there is a species of Dixie darling who can be overheard saying, "Thank you for comin' over and fixin' the air conditioner, baby. Why don't you lean back and let Mama clean your pipes." I just didn't know these women could be found on the faculty of the Women's Studies Departments at our most prestigious universities.

Forget gender studies, feminists need to go back to Logic 101 and work their way back from the heartland of their new Redneck Nation.

13

Taken to the Extreme

I have seen the future of southern-style evangelicalism and it's an angry lesbian vegetarian who wants to take away your cell phone.

Of all the bad habits of the Old South that you Yankees could pick up, the last one I expected would catch your eye is Prohibitionism. Folks misspeak when they talk about southern puritans. Puritans are a New England invention. We Southerners are Prohibitionists, a far higher calling. Puritanism, as Mencken noted, is the fear that someone, somewhere, may be having a good time. Prohibitionism is the need to track that person down and bludgeon him into submission.

You can find the skeletal remains of the twentieth-century Prohibition movement scattered across the legal landscape of the South: blue laws, dry counties, and—a hometown favorite of mine—minibottles. When people from civilized climes travel to South Carolina, they inevitably stare in astonishment at the little airplane bottles from which their liquor drinks are served. Instead of pouring a shot of their favorite hooch from a liter bottle, the bartender is required by law to crack open a 1.5-ounce mini. The confused tourist glances about to check if his bar stool is locked in its upright position. The minibottles are a hassle for the bar owners, an annoyance for the servers, and—if he's ordering any multiliquor beverage like a Long Island Iced Tea—wildly exorbitant in price for the customers.

"What's the point?" thirsty travelers slumped over their Bourbon and branch waters want to know, and it's a good question. Today, South Carolina clings to minibottles for the added revenue to state coffers these higher-priced drinks generate. But the real purpose was to keep Prohibition alive.

Back in the early 1970s, one of the great debates in southern states was what to do about "liquor by the drink," which, as any southern Baptist will tell you, is as dangerous to your mortal soul as lottery by the ticket or sex by the hour. These folks were content with the old BYOB bottle-club system and the attendant hindrances that came with toting your own liquor.

It was a royal pain in the neck, and many bars and restaurants decided to take their chances with John Law and mixed drinks, anyway. This was a problem. The law was being flouted and the legislators from these Baptist districts knew it, having spent a few nights passed out on the floors of these speakeasies themselves.

They couldn't go back home to the voters and legalize their own elbow-bending because the voters wouldn't have it. But they couldn't sit back while perfectly good tax dollars poured into the pockets of bar owners, either. The compromise was to continue to force drinkers to still buy their own bottle, as they did in the bottle clubs, only now the bottle would be very, very small.

Voilà—the minibottle. A solution to the problem of public vice that was simple, obvious . . . and dumb.

The grip of this Prohibitionist spirit continues in the dry counties of Tennessee, the bottle clubs of Kansas, and the minibottles in Myrtle Beach, South Carolina. These citizens simply aren't prepared to accept individual liberty in its many, glorious forms. Southern conservatives love to mock Senator Hillary Rodham and her mantra that "it takes a village to raise a child," but their willingness to police the corner pub and rural roadhouse shows they agree with her at heart.

This "your business is my business" ethos was ever present in the South of my youth. It never occurred to either the libationist or the little old lady trying to knock the julep out of his hand that his decision to drink and the bar's decision to serve him were nobody else's concern. A libertarian down South is as out of place as a hot dog stand at a PETA convention. The drunk leaning against the bar in Gadsden, Alabama, knows he's going to burn in Hell one day and he's grateful for the efforts of his neighbors—however annoying—to pull him back from the awaiting fires.

Northerners scratch their heads in confusion at this redneck naiveté. What kind of self-righteous, judgmental people put up such ridiculous roadblocks between a legal business selling a legal product and adults of legal age who choose to buy it? Northerners can't imagine such overbearing Prohibitionists in the twenty-first century.

They should imagine California.

If you traveled back in time to the 1920s and told the

folks in a New York speakeasy that a free, full-grown American in the twenty-first century isn't allowed to smoke a cigarette in a barroom, they would curse the Nineteenth Amendment and assume that the Bible Belt had somehow gotten wrapped around Uncle Sam's throat. Banning all cigarettes? The fast fellas and flappers of old New York would curse the Bible-thumpers of the fallen Confederacy and blame the noxious idea on southern Prohibitionists.

And they would be right, at least in spirit.

The Smoke Nazis currently prowling America's landscape are as redneck in their approach as Carrie Nation with her mighty ax. They have taken the fundamentalist leap from "You ought not do that" to "And I've got to find a way to stop you!" The same northern sophisticates who snicker at the very idea of bottle clubs are the ones who support forcing smokers into private smoking clubs to keep their sinful cigarettes from the eyes of children, soccer moms, and other weak-minded citizens.

I know what you're thinking: "But, Michael, cigarettes are bad! They serve no useful purpose! And they endanger others! We don't care if some poor soul wants to give himself lung cancer, but he's got no right to be a menace to others!"

Believe me, I've heard it all before. In fact, every Southerner who's cast a vote for a county option alcohol ordinance has heard it. There isn't a single new argument from the finger-pointing Prohibitionists, North or South, and none of these arguments can overcome the libertarian (I used to say "northern") principle that it's none of your damn business.

You can believe, and rightly so, that smoking cigarettes

will kill smokers. You can further believe—though the evidence is hardly conclusive—that someone smoking a cigarette will kill you. But to get from these two propositions to "It should be a crime for a bar to allow its customers to smoke," you must make a ridiculous leap of Prohibitionist faith to the idea that grown-ups simply should not be allowed to decide how to get along.

Why isn't the entire issue solved by letting the bar owner hang a sign outside that says, *"Warning:* This establishment owned by Satan and his minions in the Republican National Committee. Those who enter are encouraged to smoke, drink, play cards, make jokes about sex, and read the editorial page of the *Wall Street Journal.* Enter at your own risk!" What more is required? No one need patronize the bar who doesn't choose to, employment at such an establishment cannot be mandated, and if there is no customer demand, market forces will soon convert the site into a shop for holistic medicines or a retailer of government-issued lottery tickets.

CALLING ALL YANKEES!

There are certain forms of Prohibitionism indigenous to the various regions. In the South, our attention-grabbing antics are more quixotic and entertaining, but they are far less dangerous than the earnest idiocy of our northern neighbors. Take, for example, the decision by the state of New York to ban the use of handheld cell phones while driving. Southerners may be dumb, but we're not stupid. At least, not *that* stupid.

When we saw the poll numbers showing that 85 percent of New Yorkers supported a prohibition on cell phone use, we Southerners just shook our heads and muttered, "Only in New York." First of all, if 85 percent of the state's drivers really feel that way, they don't need a law. They just need to put down their cell phones. Problem solved.

But these days it is more often Northerners who allow the government to deny the rights of all because of the foolish behavior of the few, and to be celebrated by the majority for doing so. We aren't as willing to ban cell phone use down South, where people unable to drive and talk at the same time used to be called dumb.

Now we call them New Yorkers.

Are some citizens incapable of driving safely while carrying on a conversation? Of course. What the new Prohibitionists are laughably unable to grasp—but that we Southerners understand very well—is that stupid people will reveal their stupidity in their actions, not their technology.

If New Yorkers really want safer highways, they won't arrest people for using a device that might one day distract from their driving. They will arrest people for the bad driving they do while actually distracted. Any driver weaving from lane to lane, running stop signs, and tailgating is a menace to be stopped, regardless of what causes the bad driving. What difference does it make if this dangerous driver is talking on a phone, reading a book, or buttering a bialy?

The South has long been considered a more superstitious, less rational region of the nation. But no southern legislature would approve such a totemic ban on "evil" objects like cell phones. A driver who plowed into a tree and then said, "It wasn't me, Officer, it was this bad, bad talkin' machine," would be laughed right out of Dixie.

But Prohibitionists can't wait around for you to do something harmful, because they don't believe you have the right to be bad in the first place. Instead, they see the government as the proper agency to make you be good.

VEG OUT

I truly understand the desire to coerce one's neighbors into righteousness. Part of growing up in the South is knowing that your neighbors will always be there to comment on what you do, as though it is somehow their business.

One summer during my college years, I came home from the confines of Oral Roberts University and grew a beard—in direct contravention of Oral's orders. It wasn't much of a beard, rather thin and scruffy, but I was proud of it. What fascinated me was the willingness of total strangers to comment on it. One older lady whom I had never met actually stopped me to say, "You know, you'd look pretty good if you'd get rid of that beard." I remember thinking at the time, "What kind of nosy, obnoxious busybodies are we down here? This kind of thing never happens up North."

Then I met a vegetarian.

I am not saying you have to be annoying to be a vegetarian. Only if you want to be really good at it.

Few people are more unbearable than the Vegetarian of Virtue, the tirelessly evangelical eschewer of flesh. He cannot let a public meal go by without casting judgment on the victuals. As each dish is presented, he issues his pronunciamentos on the congregation of comestibles: "Fish: mild backsliding. Chicken: not for the true believer. Veal—Let the Lord rain fire from above!"

These vegheads are in a class apart from the casual vegetarian who avoids meat eating for reasons of health, nutrition, or weight loss. This vegetarian is, from an animal-rights standpoint, the moral equivalent of a Christmas and Easter Christian: He wants the benefits of righteousness without the disquieting irrationalism of the faith. He is not a true believer.

Neither is the handful of unfortunate souls who claim they just don't like the taste of meat. I've actually met one or two of these people, and they truly amaze me. They insist that meat simply doesn't taste good to them, that if they were seated at Patout's in New Orleans and presented with a smoked filet mignon topped with sautéed crawfish and slathered in a cream reduction sauce, they would greet it with a yawn and order a spinach salad.

These people aren't stupid. They're ill. They need our help and our prayers.

My disdain is reserved for the moral vegetarian alone. Moral vegetarianism is a form of religious extremism, not dissimilar from the extremism I lived with at Oral Roberts. But unlike ORU, whose dictates were confined by biblical literalism, veganism is a religion without theology, without (to paraphrase Al Gore) any controlling moral authority. The result is a group of radical activists who believe it is wrong to eat a chicken and okay to burn down a KFC to make that point.

Why isn't it enough for you to stop eating meat? Why must you attempt to coerce me into your dismal, dietary hell? But the spirit of Prohibitionism is too strong. I watch the political battle over public smoking and I see the eyes of the vegans light with hope: today the Marlboro, tomorrow the meat loaf!

Even vegetarians I like are almost unbearable company. Years ago I was having dinner with Kathy Najimy, the wonderfully talented comic actress. We have a mutual friend who introduced us after a performance of the hysterically funny *Kathy and Mo Show* in New York, and we all met for dinner in Greenwich Village.

I didn't know Kathy very well, but when my dinner came, she didn't hesitate to hit me with the Vegan War Cry: "You're not going to *eat* that, are you?"

I looked down. In front of me was a plate of skewered chicken. On each side, a fork and knife. What other possible outcome, I wondered, did she have in mind?

"You really shouldn't eat that," she intoned, exasperated. "Eating meat is so unnatural."

And so it begins, the Prohibitionist arguments against my choice to slap a rump roast on the barbie. And like the southern Prohibitionists, the arguments of the New Age nannies are uniformly weak.

What, for example, could possibly be "unnatural" about eating meat? Human beings are mammals. We are bipeds. And we are omnivorous. There is nothing more natural in this world than an omnivore (me) sitting down to a heaping plate of flora and fauna. A cursory examination of our species finds incisors at the front end and a large intestine at the back. Baby, I was built for beef!

Still, she wouldn't stop. I have since discovered that militant vegetarians never stop. They're like Mormons . . .

except Mormons don't smell like bean curd and they at least feel some vague, moral duty to be polite.

Not the vegheads. They come straight at you, and it's almost always with the same arguments, the catechisms of the anticarnivore. I've had dozens of discussions with vegans, vegheads, and animal-rights activists of varying passion and intellect, and they always come back to the same questions:

NUMBER ONE: Don't you know meat is bad for you?

No, I don't know it. My doctors don't know it, the Food and Drug Administration doesn't know it, and millions of years of human evolution don't know it. But vegetarians are incessant in their demand that you agree with them that meat is inherently unhealthy.

I actually knew one stand-up comic who was a vegetarian alcoholic. He smoked pot and drank beer all day, but wouldn't eat a hamburger because "all meat is bad for you." Four ounces of beef aren't any worse for you than twelve ounces of beer, and the fact that this lush had dedicated his life to the pursuit of cirrhosis of the liver was not an argument for the elimination of alcohol from the American diet. But because vegans are zealots, they insist that you see every bite of bologna as an irreparable moral failing.

NUMBER TWO: Don't you believe that all killing is wrong?

The second test of the church of Save the Chickens is even dumber than the first. Of course, all killing isn't wrong. If it were, every house cat in America would be facing the chair (an idea I fully favor, by the way). Animals kill each other all the time. It's called the food chain, and there is no substitute. Are all the dead mice, fish, birds, and gazelles killed in the wild victims of a crime? If so, what do you vegans intend to feed the millions of fish, fowl, and fast-moving felines who live off of flesh? At this point, the argument inevitably turns to . . .

NUMBER THREE: Yes, but people don't have to kill to live. Since we have the moral sense to tell us right from wrong, isn't it wrong for *us* to kill?

And thus, tenet three reveals that veggie-ism is nothing more than redneck evangelicalism wrapped in radicchio and served on a bed of kelp.

The folks back home who wanted to take away my right to "drink, smoke, or chew, or run with women who do" founded their Prohibitionism in their faith. Now I've got militant vegetarians attempting to do the same thing. They appeal to my "moral sense," which conveniently allows them to avoid making any appeals based on biology or reason.

But this argument against meat eating ends up in a traffic circle of logic. Either I'm just another animal making my way on the Good Lord's earth, as some vegheads argue, in which case I have just as much right to eat my fellow animals as they have to eat me; or I have a metaphysical moral sense, in which case I am a higher being and have been given dominion over the animals on the earth and the birds in the air just like the Good Book says. Either way, I win! Fire up the grill!

I cannot recall a conversation with a militant vegetarian that did not leave me embarrassed on his behalf. And I can't recall a single one who had the sense to be embarrassed for himself. If anything, they continue to evangelize their vacuous worldview even more fervently.

If there was any doubt about the Prohibitionist nature of the animal-rights movement, it was resolved after the

September 11 attacks. That's when Karen Davis, Ph.D. of United Poultry Concerns, made this public statement:

"For 35 million chickens in the United States alone, every single night is a terrorist attack. . . . The people who died in the [World Trade Center] attack did not suffer more terrible deaths than animals in slaughterhouses suffer every day. Moreover, the survivors of the September 11 attack and their loved ones have an array of consolations—patriotism, the satisfaction of U.S. retaliation, religious faith, TV ads calling them heroes, etc.—that the chickens . . . do not."

And you think the Christian Coalition is extreme?

If you view the world as Ms. Davis does, however, you must take action. Just as the southern Prohibitionist believes the next drink will send your soul to damnation, Davis knows that poultry must be preserved, protected, and honored. Given the lack of religious faith noted by Ms. Davis, perhaps these hedonistic hens should be evangelized as well.

I, for one, would be happy to declare all chickens heroes, to give them official military status, and allow them the practice of the religion of their choice if it would make Ms. Davis happy.

Somehow, I think not.

14

Blowed Up Real Good

F rom the sports pages:

> ARJAY, Ky. (Reuters)—A Kentucky man who accidentally killed his best friend when he took up his dare to shoot a beer can off his head was being held Tuesday on murder charges, police said. Assault charges against Silas Caldwell, 47, were upgraded to murder after his friend, Larry Slusher, died from the head wound. Witnesses told police the two had been drinking when Slusher posed the dare and Caldwell took him up on it, firing a .22-caliber semiautomatic pistol.

If the first Olympic Games had been held in Athens, Georgia, instead of Athens, Greece, Larry Slusher would be a gold medal athlete.

For any sport, game, or competitive activity to become a popular southern pastime it must adhere to two principles: The rules must be very simple and easy to understand, and there must be at least a theoretical chance that at some point during the event, someone or something is "gonna get blowed up real good."

A good example is cockfighting, which once did boffo box office down South. It's easy enough—two angry gamecocks try to kill each other—and there is guaranteed bloodshed. Cockfighting has become rare, even in the deepest South, due to the fact that it is both illegal and (speaking from experience) painful. But the popularity of simplistic, dangerous pastimes continues to dominate entertainment in the South.

I learned this aspect of southern character when, as a young teen, my cousin Joey challenged me to a game of Throw the Knife. Once again, the rules were simple: Joey handed me his hunting knife, with a four-inch blade, spread his feet about shoulder-width, and waited for me to throw the knife at his feet, the object to leave it quivering ninja-style in the ground between his ankles. Then he picked up the knife and did the same to me. Whoever got closer to the other person's foot without drawing blood won. Or to describe the game another way: If I stick a four-inch knife into your foot, you would consider that a good thing.

Note that Joey, a true, 100 percent Southerner, suggested that I be the one to throw the knife first, a touch of chivalry worthy of comment. Southerners aren't looking for an excuse to hurt somebody else; they just want to see someone or something get hurt—even themselves. My southern youth was one long pursuit of entertainment through the manipulation of pain, minor tortures, and the threat of fatality. Joey and I watched to see who would hold the firecrackers the longest as their fuses sparked and spit; when Uncle Joe pulled his pickup into the long driveway, we tried to jump out of the back as early as we dared, before he slowed down; we would jump onto tractors rolling through a field with the hay baler roaring behind.

These were my southern Summer Olympic Games in a community where previous competitors like Stumpy, Lefty, and One-Eyed Earl were our legendary champions.

Perhaps that's why it was in Tennessee that a gang of college freshmen hanging around in the vacant campus library thought "it would be a thrill to leap into a small opening they thought was a laundry chute," according to the Darwin Awards website. It didn't occur to the first jumper that few libraries actually provide fluff 'n' fold laundry service until he slid three stories and found himself in an automatic trash crusher.

Most of him was found there the next day.

And it was an Alabama man who died of rattlesnake bites—the hard way. He and a friend were tossing the poisonous reptile in a round of that popular southern game Catch the Rattlesnake. The friend was merely hospitalized and therefore is now widely suspected of being a Yankee.

It was a Knoxville, Tennessee, teenager who read in a porn magazine that a cow's heart, with its wide valves and suction capacity, may be converted into an organic sex toy with the proper application of electric current. Unfortunately for the deceased, 110 volts directly out of the wall socket was significantly above the manufacturer's specifications. Then again, if the goal of great sex is to "see Jesus," he succeeded.

And it was a twenty-two-year-old Virginia man with a large supply of accessory straps and plenty of time on his hands who headed to a seventy-foot-high railroad trestle in Fairfax County. Accessory straps are those little "bungee cords" used to strap things on top of your car, and the Virginian had the brilliant idea of taping several of the straps together. Then he wrapped one end around his foot, the other end to the trestle . . . and jumped. His body was recovered on the pavement seventy feet below. It was at the end of approximately eighty feet of homemade cord.

Yes, stupidity is America's true national pastime, and similar stories can be told from Long Beach, California, to Long Island, New York. But when you read a headline, "Man Killed in Friendly Ax-Catching Contest," what's the dateline going to read—above the Mason-Dixon line or below it? Is the tendency to convert dangerous idiocy into recreational activity a northern trait or southern?

Simple, savage, and stupid—these are the hallmarks of redneck entertainment. Sure, the drunk guy with the empty Budweiser on his head yelling, "Go ahead, Silas— shoot!" could be an aberration. But what about the fact that he lives in a place where the sacred words of the weekend are "rasslin', racin', and runnin' that football"?

It may be impossible to overstate the southern enthusiasm for football. Sportswriter Grantland Rice summed it up, "In the East, football is a cultural exercise, on the West Coast, it's a tourist attraction, in Texas it's a big get together, in the Midwest it's a slugfest. But in the South, it's a religion." In my humble opinion, Mr. Rice may overestimate our devotion to the southern Baptist Convention. Football a mere religion? Many of my fellow Southerners would convert to Islam and clad their women in burkas if it meant an NCAA football championship.

Of course, there are plenty of basketball and baseball

fans down South, but football is in a sporting and social class of its own. Thanks to programs like those at Duke and UNC, folks think basketball is big-time down South, but in fact only two southern states (Tennessee and Kentucky) produce NCAA basketball players at a per-capita rate higher than the national average.

The same is true of baseball, which is truly stunning given the climatic advantages. Only Florida and Alabama (barely) produce more than an above-average number of big-time baseball players despite the advantage of year-round baseball weather. This is analogous to Canada producing the same percentage of hockey players as Cuba, or the San Francisco Bay Area exporting a below-average number of antiwar protesters.

It is only in football that the South outperforms the nation. As John Shelton Reed points out in *1001 Things Everyone Should Know About the South*, "Where else would a house-and-garden magazine like *Southern Living* pick an all-star football team?" America's three biggest states for per capita production of major college and pro football players are Texas, Mississippi, and Louisiana, and every southern state is above the national average. They may wear the colors of Nebraska and Notre Dame, but they grew up under the St. Andrew's cross.

Football fealty is such a component of southern culture that my lack of it alone was enough to bring my Confederate bona fides into question. I never cared much for football because I never played much of it. My high school was too small to have a football team until my senior year. Before that, if a group of eleven black guys was ever spotted in a huddle in my hometown, the local constabulary would turn the dogs and hoses on them.

Still, I was exposed to enough football fever to break out in an occasional fall sweat. Because I grew up not far from the University of South Carolina, I am ostensibly a Gamecock fan, which is convenient given that until the arrival of Coach Lou Holtz, the USC Gamecocks were only ostensibly a football team. After getting married and returning to South Carolina, I started going to USC football games again, if only to watch tens of thousands of normally inhibited southern ladies shout "Go Cocks!" in public.

It is very important, by the way, that I identify myself as a Gamecock fan, so that I may be differentiated from our evil, in-state rivals, the Clemson Tigers. Clemson was founded as South Carolina's agricultural college, and its fans are illiterate, thick-necked chaw-spitters who send Father's Day cards to their brothers. Oh, yeah: Clemson also won some kind of NCAA football championship or something, but the whole team was later arrested, so who cares?

The Gamecocks, on the other hand, are whiny, limp-wristed frat boys waiting to join their daddy's law firm. They don't know a jockstrap from a training bra and only have a football team so real schools will have someone to play on homecoming weekend.

Almost every southern state has a similar college-sport social divide that separates the white collars and the blue collars on Saturdays. In Tennessee, the rednecks holler for Tennessee and the bookworms bellow for Vandy. In Georgia, it's not just the jerseys that are red at Georgia, while locals with fantasies about MIT wear Georgia Tech jackets of yellow. In Mississippi, it's Ole Miss versus State; in North Carolina, it's Duke versus everyone else; and in

Arkansas, it's the Razorbacks versus the Little Rock School of Plumbing. You decide which one is for the intellectuals.

From a sociological standpoint, it's also interesting to note that college football in the South has far more fans than alumni. The stands are filled, not with graduates, but with locals who have pledged their devotion based on what the decision to support that specific school says about themselves.

You can see the devoted fan slouched before his morning papers each Sunday, a grown man's self-worth completely invested in the ability of some nineteen-year-old kid to kick an oblong ball in a straight line. As the fan's team goes, so goes his morning, his week, his life. A pummeling of the home team by in-state rivals leaves him as dejected as a busted Vegas gambler on the last bus home. A come-from-behind victory, and he is the king of all he surveys.

The result is that the non-alums are far more ferocious in defense of their U. than the students are. Is this hypocritical? Sure it is. But so is college football. The school administrators and coaching staff all pretend that their football team consists of "scholar athletes" playing a little ball between biology labs and philosophy lectures. Meanwhile, the fans know that the NCAA is just the NFL's minor league, that most of the grunting, hormonal growths on the field couldn't make their way through an issue of *Field & Stream* without tutoring. Northerners who say the South isn't much on football because we have so few "professional" teams are clearly unfamiliar with the financial incentive programs at Alabama, Miami, and the now-defunct Southwestern Conference.

I have suggested to many die-hard football fans in the South that we end this charade, stop torturing these poor, dumb kids, and just let them play ball for the school of their choice at a reasonable salary. The athletes will make a little money, and the Graduate School of Business can close all those sections of Dilbert as Literature 101.

Southerners reject this notion out of hand. That's not our vision of "playin' baw-ull." We have a sincere desire to honor the noble efforts of amateurs untouched by the mercenary motives of professionals, and this desire infuses our football loyalties with great meaning. And the fact that our vision of college football is completely and obviously false shouldn't stop us. We're Southerners: Ignoring the obvious is one of our proudest traditions.

Part of my rejection of my southern roots involved turning my back on football and culturing an affectation for baseball. I made myself a baseball fan, though I had never been to a professional game and had never even watched a full nine innings on TV until I was in my late twenties. I did this because baseball was, I thought, the national pastime of the North. It was the national pastime somewhere, I was repeatedly assured by Bob Costas and others, but it sure wasn't down South.

When Hollywood made sports movies, the sport of choice was baseball. When politicians waxed poetic upon their youth, they would recall the Washington Senators or the first time they saw Mickey Mantle play. And when entertainers I admired like Bill Murray or Billy Crystal talked sports, it was baseball—memories of Yankee Stadium or the Green Monster in Boston or Tiger Stadium in Detroit (where I saw my first major league game). The only sport

that has tempted me into impassioned fandom as an adult
is baseball.

Try to imagine George Will and George Mitchell debating the finer points of hockey. It cannot be done.

If there were passionate baseball fans in South Carolina, they were kept sedated. Pro baseball didn't come to
the Deep South until the Milwaukee Braves were dragged
to Atlanta, and a precious few Southerners even noticed
until Ted Turner put their games on the Superstation. I recall sitting in a bar during the Braves miracle season of
1991 trying to watch a play-off game. Two of my fellow
Southerners kept trying to get the channel changed to pro
football. When I suggested politely that a play-off game
and a chance to go to the freakin' World Series was of
some import, one of them replied, "I'm not much of a
baseball fan. Too intellectual."

Baseball? Intellectual? Intellectuals in America used to
be people who debated epistemology and the nature of
being. Today, they contemplate existential issues raised by
the infield fly rule.

I have heard this sentiment expressed frequently since
then, though never so shamelessly. Baseball requires the
spectator to pay attention, to think ahead. And while there
are occasional home plate collisions and wild pitches,
there's little likelihood of significant bloodshed. Needless
to say, it's not very popular down South. The only reason
there is any Major League Baseball down South at all is
that every New Yorker over the age of seventy now lives
in Florida.

It should be painfully obvious at this point that I am ignoring two pillars of southern sports, wrestling and
NASCAR. I am ignoring them because, well, that's been a

policy of mine since achieving adulthood, and it has served me well. But when you grow up in a house within ten minutes of both a dirt stock car track and a wrestling school/convenience store (I swear to God, on Highway 302 just outside Pelion), it's hard to do.

Making fun of pro wrestling today is passé, but back home, mocking Chief Wahoo McDaniel and Ricky "the Dragon" Steamboat was a health hazard. At the time, TV wrestling wasn't available in many markets up North, and even in the South it was relegated to Saturday afternoons on UHF stations, but its followers were a devoted lot. They watched every move, they followed every plot line, and, as I learned from beneath the three-hundred-pound son of one of my dad's coworkers, they were constantly looking for someone to practice on.

In my circles, wrestling was more popular than NASCAR, which wasn't called NASCAR but just "racin'" or "the race." I remember my father taking me to Darlington to see Richard Petty (if you have to ask "Where's Darlington?" you should just skip the rest of this chapter). I was about seven years old and had never even heard the word "redneck," but after two hours in that crowd I was struggling to come up with it. Here were tens of thousands of people who understood the physics of air movement, the chemistry of fuel ignition, and the algebra of restrictor plates, but who probably could not operate a manual toothbrush.

From my first encounter with car racing, I hated it. I actually met Richard Petty that day and got his autograph on a program, but I was happy to get back from the speedway alive. The longer I lived in the South and the more popular racing became there, the more my loathing increased. One of the many benefits of leaving the South, I thought at the time, was the distance I was putting between me and everyone who had Charlie Daniels in the tape deck and an artist's rendition of Calvin urinating on a numeral painted on his or her truck.

Good-bye, wrasslin', racin', and rednecks, I told myself as I headed North, and hello, America! Buy me some peanuts and Cracker Jacks at the ol'—ball—g-a-a-a-m-e!

Which is why I am so proud to report that America's fastest-growing and most popular spectator sport today is. . . . NASCAR Winston Cup stock car racing! *Aaaagghhh!*

Let me get something off my chest right now, my fellow redneck Americans: *NASCAR is not a sport.* It is a game, yes. It's a contest, a competition of skill, of course. But it is *not* a sport!

A sport is an athletic competition. NASCAR is a skill competition, like bowling or lawn darts . . . except that in lawn darts there is little chance your opponent is going to slam into you at 200 mph and burst into a fireball. If he does, I suggest you forfeit the match.

In an athletic·competition, all other factors being equal, athleticism will determine the outcome. Which is why, by the way, golf is not a sport. Put down the putter, Tiger, and calm down. I'm not saying golf is bad, or that it's not a worthwhile game. I'm simply pointing out that any activity in which John Daly can be a champion is clearly not a competition among athletes.

A sport is fundamentally a contest of the flesh, and NASCAR is a contest of machines. The strongest driver is not significantly more likely to win than the weakest driver, but the strongest car always has the biggest edge.

Yes, NASCAR drivers need amazing skill and tremendous concentration, and, yes, they get out of the cars hot, sweaty, and tired. But if we had the American Speed Typing championships in an un-air-conditioned warehouse in Georgia, the effects would be the same. Would that make typing a sport?

The fact that NASCAR isn't a sport doesn't mean that it isn't worth watching. No, the fact that it is a redundant, repetitive, pointless spectacle completely unconnected in any way to our lives is the reason NASCAR is the biggest waste of time this side of the luge. And Americans cannot get enough of it.

More tickets were sold for NASCAR events in 2000 than for any other sportslike event in America. NASCAR has a six-year, $2.4-*billion* broadcasting deal with Fox, NBC, and TBS. During the economic downturn of 2000–2001, and despite an eighty-dollar average ticket price—higher than baseball, basketball, or football—NASCAR's Winston Cup races typically put a minimum of 135,000 people into the stands. There are new tracks going up all the time, not in Charlotte or Talladega, but in Chicago, New Hampshire, and Kansas.

NASCAR is a contest in which a whole lot of nothing happens, much of it at 200 mph. The true vacuity of NASCAR is revealed by a typical broadcast of the Performance Radio Network, which covers Winston Cup and other racing events on its 450 affiliates in Deep South states like Wisconsin and Vermont. If you think it's boring watching guys drive cars in circles for three hours, you ought to try *listening* to it sometime: "And they're going in a circle, and it's a circle, and another circle and another . . . and they're turning left, and left, and another left and they're turning left again . . ."

Of course, they're turning left! They're never going to turn right! Ever! It's NASCAR—it's the same guys doing the same thing over and over again for five hundred miles. NASCAR on the radio is as stupid as Olympic diving on the radio: "Oooh, look at that splash—oh wait, you can't. It's on the radio." Who is listening to this? Who is watching it? Who cares?

You do. The reason NASCAR is America's number one live spectator sport is that we are now an entire nation of people waiting for something to get "blowed up real good" and NASCAR is the only event that mixes hot metal, flammable liquids, and human flesh. When nothing goes wrong and everyone makes it home alive, NASCAR does well. When something goes wrong and a driver doesn't make it home, NASCAR does even better.

The death of Dale Earnhardt in 2001 made NBC, Fox, and TBS rich and NASCAR's owners, the France family of Daytona Beach, even richer. Ratings were up about 30 percent midway through the season, and revenues from ticket sales and merchandise were way up, too.

The wreck at Daytona that killed Earnhardt placed a death mask right on the face of NASCAR, and a clown mask on its biggest fans. Earnhardt's death was a tragedy, as all such deaths are, but I was unswayed by those who breathed solemnly that Earnhardt "died doing what he loved best." No, I bet if we could speak to him, he'd say that he loved going home to his family every Sunday even more.

Dale Earnhardt was out on that track specifically to satisfy the entertainment desires of his fans, who wanted to see him and the other drivers face death for their entertainment. That is the engine that drives NASCAR, the source of the excitement. Disagree? Ask yourself this question: If new radar, computer-controlled technology could be employed to take over the controls of a car in the event of an imminent collision, guaranteeing that there would never, ever be another wreck in a NASCAR event, what would that do to attendance at the next race?

Let's put it this way: There would be bigger crowds for the Bob Jones University Theater's touring production of *Othello*.

American NASCAR fans don't want anyone to get hurt (with the possible exception of Jeff Gordon), but they do want to see people drive really fast and crash into each other. And since these fans know what a crash can mean at 200 mph, they are essentially waiting for someone to be hospitalized. Or worse.

Which is what made the national outpouring of faux grief over the death of Dale Earnhardt so nauseating. Churches, chapels, and funeral homes across the nation held special services for NASCAR folks so the same people who leered over the wall at every spinout and wipeout could cry their eyes out surrounded by fellow gawkers. The maudlin sentimentality came in doses so strong even country music fans found it hard to stomach. One mourner in Goose Creek, South Carolina (approximately three hundred miles from any connection whatsoever to Dale Earnhardt), said that the rain falling on their ceremony was "the angels cryin' for Dale," and another said she thought she saw Dale's number 3 in the clouds that night.

This is America's fastest-growing pastime? The equivalent of "Hey, let's get a bunch of guys, drive as fast as we can, and see who wrecks first, whattaya say? Maybe some-

thin' will blow up!" What's the substantive difference between this and my cousin Joey's knife game, or Catch the
Rattler or even "Betcha can't shoot this offa my head"?

Watching NASCAR lap other sports in popularity
wouldn't be so hard if it were an aberration, but alas, no.
Check out the ratings on cable TV for the past decade and
you'll see that in a typical week, five or more of the top
ten shows were wrestling—a program where grown men
dress up in costume, climb into a dog pen, and pretend
to beat each other up with furniture. Wrestling is getting
nervous, however, because it's losing ratings to shows like
Fox's *Tough Man* competitions on their FX network,
where grown men actually *do* beat each other up with
furniture, or whatever they can get their hands on. In the
lead up to the Super Bowl in 2002, FX broadcast a special
edition of *Tough Man* called "The Tough Bowl," featuring
former NFL greats (Anthony Munoz), near greats (Ickey
Woods), and great big fat losers (William "the Refrigerator"
Perry). Here's how sportswriter Jamey Codding described
the action between Ickey Woods and Billy Sims:

> The bell sounds, and these two fly out of their re-
> spective corners like two Tazmanian Devils, throw-
> ing wild punch after wild punch after wild punch.
> Uppercuts, roundhouses, jabs, haymakers . . . Ickey
> and Sims both unleashed their entire arsenal in a
> flash of uncoordinated ugliness, coming at each
> other like two off-target tornados of flailing fists. It
> all lasted about 30 seconds.

Who needs the NFL, or even the XFL? Let's just skip all
that "run, pass, and kick" and get straight to the business

of kickin' ass! Or to put it in the words of former NFLer Dexter Manley as he prepared to face off against Anthony Munoz: "I have a lot of respect for Munoz, I'm sure he's a worthy opponent. But I promise you, as sure as I'm a Negro sitting here, he's going down in two."

In case you were wondering, "FX increased viewer numbers by more than 35 percent among its target audience of adults aged 18 to 49" since it began broadcasting *Tough Man,* according to Fox officials. And, unlike NASCAR or wrestling, this event is actually a sport: human cockfighting.

In 1960, 34 percent of Americans surveyed said baseball was our national pastime—the most popular answer. Football and basketball were popular, too, and boxing was a much more important part of the American fabric than it is today. But it was baseball that we claimed as America's sport. We followed it, we talked about it, we complained about it. It was ours. The idea that it would be inaccessible, or viewed as intellectual or elitist, was unimaginable. A ten-year-old boy and his eighty-year-old grandmother could follow the season together, and they often did.

Today, baseball is on the back page. Only 13 percent of Americans call it our national pastime, according to Gallup, behind basketball (15 percent) and football (33 percent), and many of those casting a vote for baseball do so out of nostalgia. Sure, there are more baseball fans today, because there are more Americans today. But football, not baseball, is the sport that (to borrow a phrase from Bill Clinton) "looks like America." America is today where the South has been my entire life.

The difference between baseball and football is the difference between a book and a movie. You make baseball come to life by anticipating, plotting, investing yourself—what would I do? Pitch high and inside? Move up the infield? Walk Mo Vaughn and take a chance with Mike Piazza? In every baseball game, there are ten men on the field, the nine in uniform and the fan who's throwing every pitch and taking every swing up in the stands

Football is fully produced and presented to the fan, ready to serve. Football throws the action at you. It's all John Woo and no John Irving. All the fan has to do is sit back and wait to see someone's knee get blowed up real good. When the helmets (and, in Cleveland, the beer bottles) are flyin', it's a great game!

Forty years ago, families watched baseball, men watched football, and rough men indulging their baser instincts watched Sonny Liston, Cassius Clay, and the Friday night fights. Today, families watch football, men watch *Tough Man,* women love NASCAR, kids are watching other kids slam into mountains on snowboards, Mike Tyson is still allowed to box, and Southerners are trying to figure out how, in the age of political correctness, a bunch of toothless white men wearing masks, waving sticks, and beating the crap out of people suddenly regained its popularity.

Only in a Redneck Nation.

15

Hee Haw!

Call it "*throwed* up real good."

On Thursday, February 21, 2002, Fox Television served up *The Glutton Bowl: The World's Greatest Eating Competition* to a waiting, if slightly queasy, public. Dozens of "competitive eaters" chomped, choked, and gulped gallons of mayonnaise, tons of beef tongue, and fistfuls of other unpalatable foods for the chance to win a whopping $25,000—less than my local grocery store gives away each week in its bingo promotion. The folks at Fox promised a final-round surprise delicacy they described as "not for the faint of heart or weak of stomach."

It turned out to be a fifty-five-gallon drum filled with cow brains.

Now, as a Southerner I am not surprised by anything folks put in their mouths. My boyhood home was in sniffing distance of the annual Chitlins Strut held in the nearby town of Salley, South Carolina—where thousands gather to snack on that portion of the hog most susceptible to the effects of a high-fiber diet. My own grandma had a special way to cook a part of the hog she called the melt, an organ unheard-of in any butcher shop or biology book with which I am familiar. She also made headcheese, kept a barrel of cracklin' next to the stove, and whipped up a mean pot of squirrel pilau (pronounced "per-low"), a favorite of mine.

My experiences are fairly typical, which is why, in the vittles department, we Southerners don't scare easy: If you haven't eaten a handful of live bait, a huntin' dog, or another human being, we're not impressed.

And I'm not surprised that people would sit around and watch strange things getting eaten. When I was eight and working in a tobacco barn in Conway, South Carolina, I paid a quarter to see Mr. Red Winburn bite the head off a tobacco worm. Tobacco worms are green, gooey sacks of tobacco juice, a long, clingy booger of a bug, and I was eager to see a grown man— and my boss, to boot—put one in his mouth. He did it, and as he reached out to take my quarter, he taught me a valuable life lesson: A redneck will do anything for money.

When I was around twelve or so, my more rustic relatives tried to get me to eat odd, hard-to-identify, exotic items for their entertainment pleasure. The looks of anticipation around my aunt Celie's dinner table told me something was up. My uncle Teenyboy would shove a plate of some unidentifiable tissue toward me and urge me to dig in. When I asked what it was, he would cough up some backwoods euphemism straight from the Redneck Marketing Department: "Oh, them's liver and lights, they're good!" or "Why, that's a mountain oyster! What, you never had one?"

Now, I'm no Jacques Cousteau, but even I knew that "mountain" and "oyster" didn't go together. You bring me out a plate of "desert clams" and maybe we'll talk. On those occasions when my trust would overcome my reason and I would take a bite or two of the proffered delicacy, my relatives would burst into laughter and start shouting to my mother, "Pat, hey, Pat—come see what your boy done eat!" as I scurried red-faced for the nearest chamber pot. No doubt about it, watching people eat disgusting animal parts is a redneck comedy riot.

It also cracks TV's Top 20 almost every week in the good ol' U.S. of R.

You can dispute my contention that modern America is as race-obsessed as the Old South, you can reject the idea that Yankee ideals of merit and accomplishment have been superseded by the good-ol'-boy notion of "Who's your daddy?," you can even deny that NASCAR is a traditionally southern pastime that now laps the nation. But to deny that America has been 'neckified in the field of entertainment, you've got to shoot your TV, burn down the Barnes & Noble, and throw away your brain.

The Glutton Bowl may have garnered relatively modest ratings—it was up against the Olympics that night—but more significant was the lack of attention it received from finicky media critics and TV writers. Where was the outrage, Bill Bennett might ask.

Sorry, Bill. Another night, another gang of unappealing Americans subjecting themselves to bizarre tortures and humiliations for the entertainment of their countrymen. That's hardly news in the Redneck Nation.

Then . . . TV Listings, 1961

CBS, *Playhouse 90*. First-rate American writers, directors, and actors brought outstanding productions like "Requiem for a Heavyweight," "The Miracle Worker," and "The Days of Wine and Roses."

NBC, *Omnibus*. A wide-ranging ninety-minute show hosted by Alistair Cooke presenting everything from Shakespeare to golfer Sam Snead to Jonathan Winters. An eclectic mix of news stories, concerts, documentaries, operas, and comic sketches drew performers from James Dean to Charlton Heston.

ABC, the Ernie Kovacs specials. Described by many as a comedic genius, Ernie Kovacs's experimentation with television won awards and redefined the medium. One award-winning episode is the only thirty-minute television program in history with absolutely no dialogue. It was a great success.

And Now . . . TV Listings, 2002

CBS, *Survivor*. Twelve unknown, talentless Americans travel to exotic locales to undergo physical and emotional stress, eat worms, and battle for $1 million.

NBC, *Fear Factor*. People stay in the United States, undergo physical and emotional stress, eat worms, and try to win significantly less than $1 million.

ABC, *The Chair*. People get strapped into a chair, and while has-been tennis pro John McEnroe yells at them, they go through physical and emotional stress (skip the worms) and answer trivia questions with hopes of making their next three car payments.

What did I miss? What happened between 1962 and 2002 to take us from Rod Serling's *Twilight Zone* to entire TV series made up of home movies showing men being hit in the crotch? Was this the triumph of 1960s intellectualism over bourgeois American values? Or did every American spend a summer with my uncle Arthur Joe, who liked to hook an electric capacitor to a chain-link fence and watch it send yard dogs howling after they lifted their legs?

The proof of redneck media dominance isn't in the fact that television sucks. Television has always sucked. The same 1961 TV season that featured *Omnibus* and Ernie Kovacs had a minor hit called *The Hathaways,* starring Peggy Cass, Jack Weston, and a troupe of theatrical monkeys. Imagine a pre-evolutionary version of *The Partridge Family* (but with better music), and you've got the idea.

What's strange is not the badness of television, always our lowest-common-denominator medium, but rather the style and quality of the badness it currently exhibits. There are so many ways for TV to suck, who would have imagined it would suck the southern way?

In 1961, one might have predicted a television future filled with boring news shows, turgid documentaries, and self-serving conversations among pompous yet insignificant pseudo-celebrities living in Manhattan. But PBS wasn't created until the Johnson administration.

Forty years ago, one might have feared a future of bland, forgettable sitcoms, or vacuous variety shows, or nonstop westerns, or even, worst-case scenario, a national TV network based around *Hee Haw,* a wildly popular syndicated show across the South (and in the Graham household) when I was a kid. But the worst *Hee Haw*-inspired nightmares can't match the truth, the "reality," of the suckitude of modern American television. The *Hee Haw* gang may have lacked savoir faire and *je ne sais quoi,* but they never set themselves on fire, covered themselves with mucus, or videotaped the vaginal penetration of a member of the livestock family—though they were no doubt sorely tempted.

Such programming may sound like country, but it's really rock 'n roll. Or to be more precise: MTV.

MTV's *Jackass* was an entire program wholeheartedly dedicated to the traditional southern belief in the entertainment value of gross stupidity. The premise is simple: A group of young twenty-something guys hit the road in search of the line where stupidity equals death. Then they straddle that line, with tape rolling.

The head idiot—a loathsome troglodyte from Tennessee calling himself Johnny Knoxville—arranged for his pals to lie down on barbecue grills, snort worms up their noses and vomit them back out, get sprayed by skunks, attacked by bulls, beaten with guitars, and run over by various modes of transportation—naked, if possible.

Jackass was wildly popular. (As of this writing, Knoxville and Co. are producing specials and other programming for MTV to keep the nausea alive.) And, like

The Glutton Bowl, the show drew lots of viewers but little comment from media observers . . . until the ambulances arrived. At least four *Jackass* imitators harmed themselves seriously during the show's first incarnation—none of them south of the Mason-Dixon. (There was one report out of Kentucky about a young man asking his friends to run him over, but that turned out to be a local idiot who *didn't* need the inspiration of cable television to break his own neck.)

One thirteen-year-old Yankee *Jackass* wanna-be dressed up in a fire-retardant suit, covered it with steaks, and lay across a hot charcoal grill. He suffered second-degree burns. Another thirteen-year-old suffered second- and third-degree burns after two friends poured gasoline on his legs and feet and then set them on fire following the show. He was later listed in critical but stable condition in the burn unit of Boston's Shriners Hospital.

"Sure, Michael," I can hear you saying, "but those aren't rednecks, they're *teenagers.* And all teenagers are under constant assault from their glands. The fact that sixteen-year-old boys like watching people acting like idiots doesn't prove anything. They also think it's cool to have a metal stud shoved through their tongues."

To which I reply, "Pig rectums!"

No, that's not an anachronistic southern epithet. I mean, literally, porcine poopers, animal anuses, barnyard buttholes. When NBC's hit series *Fear Factor* featured close-ups of folks eating these usually discarded pork products, they snagged their highest ratings of the season. As contestants swallowed the recta down, network ratings went straight up. Not long after that, NBC had folks bobbing for chicken feet buried under a pile of live worms.

"Hey, Ma—what's in them TV dinners? Spaghetti and chicken nuggets? Yum!"

It may sound like a prime-time game show on the Deliverance Television Network, but *Fear Factor* is a jewel in NBC's broadcasting crown. It's a coast-to-coast hit with high ratings and even higher profits. It's not hard to find contestants, either. Americans from the redneck backwaters of Long Island and Detroit beg, plead, and audition for a chance to flop around in vats of rancid squid or get lowered into a tank of water snakes or lie down in the path of swarming rats (no, not the kind in charge of programming at NBC Entertainment—the short, furry kind).

In exchange, the players get the opportunity to behave repulsively on national television, demonstrate a complete lack of self-respect, and, maybe, win $50,000. Someone call my old boss Red Winburn, quick! There's a network that wants to sign you to a development deal.

Jeff Zucker, the president of NBC Entertainment, says there is a perfectly good explanation for why this network shows humans interacting with manure during prime time: "The audience wants these shows." He is absolutely right. And he's not talking about an audience limited to the residents of Terrebonne Parish, Louisiana, or the city limits of Beckley, West Virginia, either.

In the interest of fairness, let it be noted for the record that not everything on television is as bad as *Fear Factor* or *Survivor V: Trapped in the Washington, D.C., Public School System*. There are still shows celebrating intellectual vigor, like the syndicated show *Jeopardy!* and its sister program, *Wheel of Fortune,* a.k.a. *Jeopardy! for Stupid People.*

There are apparently millions of Americans astonished

by spelling, who work just as hard finding a place for a "p" in the word "pneumonia" as a typical *Jeopardy!* contestant taking "Tenth-Century Japanese Poetry for $500." And which of the two shows is the more popular?

Please. *Wheel of Fortune* holds the record for the longest-running game show to hold the number one spot in TV syndication history, nearly nine hundred weeks. Yes, nine hundred weeks of puzzled Americans staring at the missing letters in a common word or phrase and muttering to themselves, "Hmmm, Hunchback of Rotor Dame? No, Motor Dame? Maybe it's the Hunchback of Boater Dame—that's it!"

For a time, however, the monster quiz show in America was *Who Wants to Be a Millionaire?*, which slammed into the summer ratings like a tsunami in 1999. Those of us longing for more intellectually engaging TV fare took its popularity as a good sign. Sure, the questions were, shall we say, less than challenging—actual question: A person known for their fashion sense is known as a fashion (A) bowl, (B) fork, (C) saucer, (D) plate?—but at least regular folks were trying to show some mental heft. With *Millionaire*, as opposed to *Wheel of Fortune*, there was some sense that people who could answer the truly tough ones in the millionaire rounds deserved to walk away with a sack of cash. It was a show where knowledge equaled wealth, and any programming suggesting such a connection is an inherently good thing.

Not to belabor the point, but this is significant: Folks on *Millionaire* try hard not to look stupid. While *Jackass* and *Fear Factor* and *Funniest Home Videos* seemed to celebrate the idea of getting rich quick through idiocy, the contestants on *Millionaire* seem to buy into the notion that it is, in fact, possible to be too stupid. Players on *Millionaire* didn't celebrate their ignorance. They were frustrated by it.

One reason might have been the modesty of the questions. Nobody expects to know all the answers when Alex Trebek whips out the stack of cards for categories like "Infectious Diseases" and "Great Moments in Opera." But on *Millionaire,* when dopey lounge act Regis Philbin asks how many U.S. senators each state has, you can see the look of disgust on the puzzled contestant's face. "Ah, c'mon," he's thinking to himself, "I oughta know this!"

It was a small thing, a thin shaft of light, but many of us seized it as a hopeful indicator. Then *Millionaire's* ratings began to slip. The folks at ABC Television started scrambling. What was missing? What would it take to keep people watching a quiz show? Smarter contestants? Tougher questions? Topless dancers? No, wait! We've got it:

Deadly, poisonous spiders!

And thus the torture chamber quiz show was born: first ABC's *The Chair,* then Fox's *The Chamber,* and eventually, one assumes, *The Spanish Inquisition,* a joint venture of the History Channel and the S&M Network, brought to you each week by Advil and the Jesuit Society of America.

In the 1950s and '60s, quiz shows featured men and women of letters—college professors, historians, writers— to delight and amaze us with their knowledge. There was some sense that viewers wanted to be entertained by people smarter than the folks back home: Charles Van Doren, Kitty Carlisle, and the like.

The quiz show challenge today is to keep the viewer from feeling stupid, not easy in a nation where 73 percent of the public think the Gettysburg Address is the name of a new spy thriller by Robert Ludlum. So the questions can't be too tough. At the same time, watching a bunch of people answer questions like "How many digits are in your phone number . . . *without* the area code?" is hardly compelling. That's where the tarantulas come in.

On ABC's *The Chair,* contestants were strapped to a bit of furniture borrowed from a Texas gas chamber, attached to various monitors, and forced to answer questions like "Which motel chain has the sleepy bear in pajamas as its mascot?" while the producers lowered spiders into their faces or sicced alligators on them. Not only must the victims ("players" certainly isn't the right word) answer the questions, but they also had to maintain a low and steady heart rate.

Finally a TV show that combines the pleasures of a doctor's visit, the excitement of a trip to the zoo, and the intellectual challenges of your third grader's homework—now, that's what I call entertainment!

Which, actually, it is, if your standard for entertainment is shooting beer cans off your best friend's head or watching the director's-cut DVD of *Smokey and the Bandit 3.* This is precisely the dumbed-down culture I fled when I left the South. And now it's on prime time.

I remember once as a young teen sitting in our living room watching Woody Allen's *Sleeper* on ABC's Saturday night movie. Some of my dad's family were in from Horry County—a particularly rural part of South Carolina—and they were all huddled in the kitchen over a pot of coffee and hot servings of the latest family gossip. Whenever one of them came through the living room, he would stop, look at the TV screen for a minute, look at me, then shake his head and say, "What is that junk you're watching?"

How could I explain to them that this wasn't a TV program, it was a lifeline. I had never seen anything like Woody Allen before. My parents would no more have taken me to a Woody Allen movie than to a public circumcision. He was one of "them," by which they didn't mean "Jew," but much worse: "Yankee." He was some fast-talking New Yorker making fun of God, Country, and My Baby, and represented a kind of art and entertainment we had no use for.

And I loved it. I was astonished by it. I remember a few times looking around to make sure I didn't get "caught," though I couldn't say what it was I was doing wrong. I felt the way Richard Wright describes following his first encounter with H. L. Mencken:

> Why did he write like that? And how did one write like that? I pictured the man as a raging demon, slashing with his pen, consumed with hate, denouncing everything American, extolling everything European or German, laughing at the weaknesses of people, mocking God, authority. . . . It frightened me. I read on and what amazed me was not what he said, but how on earth anybody had the courage to say it. Occasionally I glanced up to reassure myself that I was alone in the room. ·

I didn't know who Woody Allen was, but I couldn't imagine how anyone could get away with these jokes about famous, important people, about religion, or especially about [stage whisper] S-E-X. And even more amazing, he was on TV. He was actually *popular.* Somewhere far from my head-shaking family was a place where Woody Allen's comedy was as well accepted around the kitchen table as "kuntry komic" Jerry Clower was around mine.

Maybe if we'd had *Jackass* when I was sixteen, I would have been a fan, who knows? When I was a teenager, I loved idiotic, counterculture, adult-annoying entertainment, too. In fact, I was (and remain) a huge fan of *Monty Python's Flying Circus,* which appeared regularly on public television in South Carolina until someone started explaining the jokes to our legislators. I read Ken Kesey and Joseph Heller and John Irving and laughed up my sleeve at the adults around me—teachers, coaches, even my very own parents—all of them ignorant of the subversive movement I had joined.

I had Steve Martin and Woody Allen and, thanks to a really hip high school band teacher, Lenny Bruce and George Carlin. For knockdown, lowbrow humor, the film *Animal House* was for me a celluloid cry for cultural revolution—hey, the drunken perverts can be the good guys!

Steve Martin was particularly influential on my decision to become a comedian because he was smart, silly, and wildly successful all at once. Steve Martin was intelligent and irrational and insightful and bizarre and gasping-for-breath funny all at the same time. He filled concert halls, he wrote goofy songs, he told jokes about philosophy, and he changed the life of a lost teenager sitting by a turntable in a small, prefab home in rural South Carolina.

In 1980, I had Steve Martin. Today, America has Carrot Top.

Should I slash my wrists now or finish this chapter?

I will refrain from insulting a fiscally successful member of my former profession other than to say that if you ever see me in the audience at a performance of Carrot Top, call the Office of Homeland Security, because it means I'm being tortured by Al Qaeda and I'm about to crack. Does comedy have to be this bad to be successful? Can't we go back to just "lame" or "mediocre"? Is excruciating stupidity really mandated by the modern American marketplace? And when did it all get so bad?

Put it into perspective: During the civil rights era, a radio tuned to a Top 40 station would occasionally play a folk song, a political protest song—even jazz artists like Dave Brubeck and Stan Kenton could be heard on radio stations not funded by taxpayer dollars. Sure, the Top 40 charts also featured songs like "Sugar, Sugar" and acts like Neil Sedaka, but it was conceivable—not likely, but at least possible—that the future of pop music in America could be challenging, complex music for thinking people who wanted to party.

But the future is now, and seven of the top ten selling CDs are either the bastard children of Britney Spears or illiterates playing sampled tracks of other people's music and screaming alliterative variations of the word "motherf******."

We've matriculated from the subtle, sly humor of the "plastics" scene in *The Graduate* to the graphic, witless comedy of the "porking the pastry" scene in *American Pie.* The sharp, social comedy of Archie Bunker and *All in the Family* has been replaced by . . . actually, there isn't anything on television today worthy of comparison.

My family and I watched *All in the Family* for years before figuring out that Archie was supposed to be the bad guy. I even had an "Archie for President" T-shirt during the 1972 campaign (looking back on the choices of Nixon and McGovern, I'm not sure it was supposed to be a joke). Like all *AITF* fans, I now constantly complain that there is nothing like it on TV today. I am frequently told by media critics and casual fans alike that—quote—"You couldn't make a show like *All in the Family* today."

Why not? Because the satire is too edgy, the unflinching honesty too discomfiting for the average American. The political windbags would blow too strongly against a show where the antagonist was stupid, bigoted, and essentially *likable*. We can't have three-dimensional characters on TV, especially racist ones. Instead, when it comes to angry white men, we get: "Hello, Central Casting? Send over some swastika-clad Klan members or a Bible-thumping bigot—and make it snappy!"

What does it say about us that the folks who tune in happily to view hours on end of bug eating, crotch kicking, and skunk spraying can't stomach thirty minutes of real-life comedy about race, politics, and society? What kind of country is it that can brave the visual onslaught of a roomful of greedy contestants eating cow brains, but is too timid to look into the mind of an Archie Bunker?

Isn't that a Redneck Nation?

Epilogue:
Confessions of a
Reluctant Southerner

W hat are you?"
Every Southerner who slips the bonds of Dixie is eventually confronted with this question of ethnic identity, a mysterious query to the one group of Americans who never had to ask. Ask someone back in rural Lexington County, South Carolina, "What are you?" and the answer's going to be "Baptist" or "Pentecostal" or "Catholic."

Okay, so it wouldn't be *Catholic* . . .

"What are you?" is a Southerner's question about church attendance, not cultural identity. When a North Carolinian asks, "What are you?" he's trying to find out if you know Jesus. When a New Yorker asks, he's looking for another way to insult you.

The question first came to me from a beautiful blond classmate at Oral Roberts University. I was making particularly ungodly advances toward her at the time, and she responded with a little impromptu Darwinism, casting a critical glance to see what I was packing in my genes.

"You're from South Carolina, so . . . what are you?"

I answered that I was Pentecostal, like most of the other students at ORU.

"NO, no, no. What *are* you?" She was demanding to know my identity, my ethnicity, what stuff was I made of.

To encourage me, Jackie, my beautiful interrogator, announced that she was Norwegian. Her mother and father back home in Minnesota were both Norwegian and her grandparents on both sides were Norwegian immigrants. "That's what I am," she told me proudly.

"Oh, okay," I replied. "I," I said with a flourish, "am white trash. My mother and father were both white trash, my dad's dad was a sharecropper and my mom's mom grew up living in a railroad boxcar. That's what I am."

"That's nothing," Jackie insisted dismissively. "That's not what you are. Where are your people from? Are they from Ireland, England, Scotland . . . ?"

"Well," I offered hesitantly, "we've been to *Grace*land. I've even got a set of 'All Shook Up' salt and pepper shakers . . ."

It was not a satisfactory answer.

Though Jackie and I began dating—we even talked about getting married at one point—the cultural differences between us were too great. The Norwegian *lefse* she brought home from Minnesota was pretty good, but *lutefisk*—the fish soaked in lye—ugh. Oh, and I fell in love with a dark-eyed soprano in the opera program, but that's another story.

Nevertheless, Jackie had a profound impact on my personal development. She left me with a question, a question I grappled with for nearly twenty years: In this era of identity politics, of ethnic division and group rights, what

is my group? In the divided, irrational, and undeniably
Redneck Nation, where do I belong? Whose team am I on?
Where are my people? What is Michael Graham?

I consider that question as I write from my new home
in Washington, D.C., the traditional boundary between
America North and South. It is ironic in a way that I have
been drawn to this area, where the southern heritage of
Virginia washes up against the concrete barrier of urban
Washington and the liberal enclave of Montgomery
County, Maryland.

Living at this intersection of American culture, I am free
to make my own alliances. I could embrace the northern
attitudes I encounter on the Metro and in the Maryland
suburbs, I could rush into the heart of this dynamic city of
D.C., or I could make camp in the northernmost reaches
of the Confederacy. The shores of the Potomac would be
the perfect place for me to remain close to, but apart from,
the South that has nurtured and nearly defeated me.

But I am not content to continue avoiding this question. I am ready to cast my lot. Twenty years, two thousand comedy club appearances, forty-one states, three
years in New York, approximately 250 pounds of mustard-
based barbecue, and some seven thousand gallons of tea
(sweet and un) later, the answer is clear:

I am a Southerner. A reluctant one perhaps, but a
Southerner nonetheless.

And I will stay one whether the South likes it or not.

I could tell you that I was a Southerner by coercion,
that like Othello I wanted to deny my birth. But I am not
a Southerner by fiat. In fact, most decent Southerners
won't claim me. They find my Confederate credentials
quite suspect. For example, I was born in Los Angeles,

where my mother, an Oklahoman, grew up. My father, who sharecropped with his father just a few miles from Myrtle Beach, South Carolina, joined the navy out of high school and was sent to Long Beach. Therefore, it could be argued, I am not a Southerner but am instead bicoastal—except that you can't tell people from down South you're bicoastal, because they think it means you have sex with men on the beach.

And I've never really acted southern. I talk fast. I ask rude questions (actually, most questions are considered rude in the South, other than "How's your mama?"). Growing up, I read books that weren't assigned by a teacher or given to me by my pastor. I listened to bebop and opera, and I've never lost a tooth opening a bottle.

No, I am not a Southerner at the insistence of the South. Trust me, most Southerners would be happy to buy me a bus ticket and point me toward Toronto.

And I don't have to be a Southerner. During my life-long struggle against Southernism, I've lived in Chicago and New York. I liked them both, and unlike most South-erners, easily fit in. I could "pass." In fact, once while liv-ing in Scarsdale, New York, someone asked me if I was Jewish.

It was one of the proudest moments of my life.

But in the ongoing discourse of my life, the painful moments of self-observation, the acute moments of self-revelation—the evidence is clear. I am a Southerner.

I am a Southerner in the same way that the Reverend Jesse Jackson is black . . . and in the same way he is a Southerner, too. I am a Southerner the same way that Flannery O'Connor was a Southerner and much the same way she was a Catholic.

I am a Southerner not because I claim it, desire it, or have somehow achieved it. I am a Southerner because after years of resistance and denial I have discovered that it is my true nature.

I confess my Southernism to underline the point that my criticism of the southernization of America is not based merely on self-loathing or the smoldering resentment of a redneck without honor in his own land. What annoys me is not that America has become more like the South, but that it has been overcome by the worst the South has to offer.

Meanwhile, there is much about the South to love, and much to my surprise, I do.

The first inkling of my deviant southern tendencies came when I was invited to lunch at the historic Chicago Racquet Club. A local whom I met through the local GOP was fascinated by my exotic Southernism and wanted to show me some true northern pride. The Chicago Racquet Club is an impressive, imposing building. Union General William Tecumseh Sherman was once a member of this club, and my host went to great pains to have us seated beneath the general's portrait in the dining room. I always enjoy a good joke and tried to play along as best I could, given that, had I been at the burning of Columbia, South Carolina, in 1865, my one comment to Sherman would have been "You missed a spot."

But as the lunch dragged on, I found myself getting more and more defensive about the South. My host's witty put-downs, which would have won my applause back home, were suddenly raising previously unworked Confederate hackles here in Chicago. By the end of the lunch, I actually found myself beginning a sentence with the words, "Well, what the Confederate flag means to me is . . ."

I stopped at two bars on my way back from that lunch.

It may be that absence makes the heart grow fonder, or it could be that I was experiencing the inverse of "familiarity breeds contempt." Whatever it was, I found myself speaking out in behalf of the South more and more. When Hurricane Fran blew through the Carolinas, a Chicagoan snickered at me, "Who wants to live in a place where you wake up one morning and your mobile home is a submarine?"

"Oh, yeah?" I shot back. "Maybe it's people who are tired of having to use butane torches to defrost their derrieres after taking a winter walk."

The low point came one day as I read the *Chicago Sun-Times*. I ran across two brief articles on the same page. The first, headlined "Anthem Anathema to US," reported that Nicaragua was considering a change in the lyrics of its national anthem for diplomatic reasons. One line giving American diplomats pause is "The Yankee is the enemy of humanity."

The next article listed South Carolina among states that have not given our nation a president. I read the article several times, and as I did, something snapped. Some vestigial Confederate organ in my brain, some recessive redneck gene, overtook me. By the time I regained consciousness, the following had been e-mailed to the *Sun-Times:*

As a South Carolinian temporarily residing in Chicago (my visa expires in November), I must respond to the scurrilous column in your vile and dis-

graceful rag which stated that South Carolina has
not given this great nation a president. Sir, that is an
outrage! You have cast a shadow upon the honor of
the Palmetto State. South Carolina gave America its
last great (true) Democratic president, Andrew Jackson. He was the greatest president since Jefferson
(another Southerner) and far superior to the
butcher, Abraham Lincoln.

The honor of the South must be restored! South
Carolina has given this nation John C. Calhoun,
Dizzy Gillespie and Lee Atwater, not to mention
hickory smoked barbecue, secession and the Shag.
The South shall rise again!

Now excuse me while I freshen up my julep.
Yours respectfully, etc. etc. PS: And what's *wrong*
with the Nicaraguan national anthem anyway?

The *Sun-Times* published a portion of my letter, and I remember reading it in disbelief a few days later. Had I really written these words? After years of denying all things
southern, was I still so completely lost in the Land of Cotton?

Apparently so. Part of the impetus for writing this book
was the unceasing barrage of arrogance and attitude di-
rected southward by northern Americans. Another motive
was to find some way to differentiate the parts of southern culture that should be buried (but sadly, have been
bought into by the rest of America) and the parts that
should be embraced and preserved.

The Northerners who have adapted the worst of Southernism have, in turn, dumped their worst upon us. Take
bagels—please.

Take them back up North or out West or wherever you brought them from. The one thing we do not need in the South is another white, flavorless breakfast starch. If I wanted to spend my mornings choking down lumps of tough, indigestible dough, I would ask my wife to start making biscuits again.

Bagels are an example of distinctly northern dining, like a bowl of clam chowder in New England or a twenty-seven-dollar plate of Chef Boyardee at a Manhattan hostaria. Bagels are about as southern as a subway token. But travel around the South and in every strip mall, in every grocery store—even in the hallowed aisles of the Winn-Dixie—there they are: bagels. And not just any bagels, either. Spreading like kudzu across the South are shops like New York Bagel and their competitors Big Apple Bagel—which is likely to be around the corner from Manhattan Bagel.

I know that the Carolinas are a popular retirement destination for disillusioned Yankees fleeing the wrecked, northern cities they helped destroy, but my God, people—didn't you leave anything behind? The New York state of mind is seizing control of the entire southern economy, and I'm not just talking delis. Down South we've got New York City Pizza, New York Life Insurance (don't they need a lot more of this than we do?), and, of course, New York Carpet World.

Without leaving our borders, I can buy a suit at New Yorker Men's Fashions, pick up a hot new frock for my favorite gal at the New York Boutique, get my hair done at New York Stylists, and while away the evening at Manhattan's Nite Life. And if that's not enough, people in Charleston, South Carolina, can go to something called

New York Moods, where, I assume from the name, cheerful Southerners can get an up-North attitudinal adjustment. I have even written them a new motto: "Turn Your Jethro into a Jerk!"

I became more sensitive than most to this new War of Northern Aggression after living in New York for a while. I can tell you firsthand that there is still plenty of northern aggression to go around. Ask a waitress in a New York restaurant if they have grits, and you might as well take out your teeth, strap on your banjo, and start squealing like a pig.

"Grits?" one particularly parochial hash slinger barked at me. "Wazzamattawitchoo? Weahdoyootinkyoare, anyway? Weahyoofum? Hey, Joey! Dis guy wants ta know if we got grits!" Well, I showed her. I hitched up my overalls, stuck my John Deere hat on my head, and stomped my bare feet outta there.

Having lived on both sides of the Mason-Dixon line, I have noticed a strange double standard. When we Southerners travel to the North and ask the locals to accommodate our cultural tastes—grits, barbecue, inbreeding—they react with indignation. "Wazzamattawitchoo? You people are weird!" Conversely, when Northerners traveling in the South find their ethnic needs occasionally unmet, their response is "Wazzamattawitchoo? You people are weird." No matter which direction you go, the blame winds up here in the South. And I believe we Southerners, beneath the weight of our regional inferiority complex, tacitly agree.

Southerners, particularly college-educated ones, are Upper West Side wanna-bes, closet carpetbaggers who believe in our hearts that we should emulate our big-city betters, with no expectation that they will return the compliment. The entire time I lived in New York, I never saw a sign for "Carolina Carpet World" or "Dixie Hairstyles." No "Alabama Boutiques" or "South Carolina Moods" either. And what's more, I didn't expect them. It seemed perfectly natural to me that New York tastes would be accommodated down South but that southern tastes would disappear in northern climates.

Southern scholars like C. Vann Woodward and John Shelton Reed place the blame on our native obsequiousness, one result of losing the war. Having lost our nation's only military "intramural scrimmage," our tendency is to defer to our northern neighbors. That is one theory.

Another, less esoteric view was best expressed by my uncle Willie: "Damn, there's a lot of Yankees! And those Catholic ones breed like rabbits." To put it another way, states like New York have big populations, and as their citizens travel, it is only natural for their superior numbers to give them more influence in the marketplace.

Whatever the cause, I believe it is time for defenders of southern heritage to respond. If America is going to be a Redneck Nation, we rednecks ought to take advantage of it while we can.

Perhaps we could get Southerners identified as an ethnic minority with special rights. The government would be forced to implement a quota system so that a certain percentage of road construction money would be set aside to build restaurants selling pecan logs along New York expressways. The National Endowment for the Arts funds could be used to foist Charlie Daniels music on unsuspecting New Yorkers. We could even ask the World Trade

Organization to impose a swap: For every bagel we eat, a Yankee has to eat a chitlin.

That'll show 'em.

My wife and I were discussing this trend with great concern not long ago, wondering what we could do to stem the tide of encroaching New Yorkism. We were down in Myrtle Beach sitting in a local watering hole at a place called Broadway on the Beach. She was drinking a Manhattan, and I was having a Long Island Iced Tea. From the jukebox came the sounds of Ol' Blue Eyes singing "New York, New York."

Suddenly it hit me. "Bartender!" I cried. "Two mint juleps—before it's too late!"